From Wolf to Wolfwood

A Genealogical and Historical Study of
the McMillans and the African American
Communities of Emory, Texas

Gwendolyn McMillan Lawe

authorHOUSE®

AuthorHouse™
1663 Liberty Drive
Bloomington, IN 47403
www.authorhouse.com
Phone: 1-800-839-8640

First published by AuthorHouse   2/11/2011

ISBN: 978-1-4567-2654-6 (sc)
ISBN: 978-1-4567-2655-3 (e)
ISBN: 978-1-4567-2656-0 (dj)

Library of Congress Control Number: 2011901885

Printed in the United States of America

Any people depicted in stock imagery provided by Thinkstock are models,
and such images are being used for illustrative purposes only.
Certain stock imagery © Thinkstock.

This book is printed on acid-free paper.

This book is dedicated to my parents, A. C. and Modis McMillan, who always supported me in all of my endeavors and gave me a rich heritage worthy of writing about and to all of the role models at each stage of my life.

Contents

Acknowledgments

There were many people who helped me in my efforts to write the manuscript for this book. Initially, it was to be just the history of the McMillans. Thanks to the guidance of Dr. James Conrad of Texas A & M University-Commerce, I expanded my research and my genealogical study became a historical study of the individuals whom I credit for my successful journey "From Wolf to Wolfwood." I was inspired by many people—some living and some I never knew—such as my great-grandparents, Alfred and Dora McMillan, Mrs. Doris Washington and Mrs. Audie Shiflet (my favorite teachers), and my inspiration for everything that I do—my husband, Theodore M. Lawe.

Foreword

From Wolf to Wolfwood chronicles the history of a family and the education of a community prior to the desegregation of schools and public facilities. More specifically, Gwendolyn McMillan Lawe, an educator reflects on her growing up in rural Emory, Texas and transitioning from a totally segregated childhood environment, and because of Brown v Board of Education and the Civil Rights Act of 1964, her becoming a student in the first integrated graduation class of her high school and then becoming a teacher in a totally integrated school district. Her educational experiences and her first teaching assignment could not have been more different. Being educated in East Texas in Rains County for an African American in the middle of the 20th Century meant attending a very small rural elementary school (a Rosenwald School) and commuting over 40 miles one-way daily to St. Paul High School, a similar Rosenwald high school in Hunt County in order to attend and graduate from high school. However, in her senior year, she attended and graduated from Rains High School in her hometown after attending only one year (1965-1966). Attending Henderson County Junior College and later receiving a Bachelor's Degree and Master's Degree from East Texas State University did not prepare her for her first job—teaching in the second largest school district in the state of Texas and teaching some of the most affluent children in the city of Dallas. However, just as she had adapted to all of her previous "new" challenges, it did not take long to find her place at her new place of employment—Hillcrest High School.

Through her research, the author validated how her family, the McMillans of Rains County, had been instrumental in the education of African Americans starting in the late 1800s through the desegregation of the schools in 1965. She discusses many of the "firsts" that she was a part of throughout her educational experiences, as well as some of the advantages and disadvantages of attending the segregated schools in her early years.

Gwendolyn McMillan Lawe chronicles how her great-grandparents, A.C. McMillan and Dora McMillan, were the first African American teachers in Emory, Texas. Her father, A.C. McMillan (named after his grandfather) was the last principal of the then all-African American school before its closing in 1969. Being born in 1948, this teacher recalls how education had always been important to her family and to the community in which she lived. It was not simply a birthright; it was something that required much effort on the part of the student as well as the community.

This publication will serve as a reminder of the days of segregation in this country, and east Texas in particular. The readers will also be able to reflect on some of the precious memories in their childhood, as well as all of the transitions made in their lives as a result of the desegregation of the schools and public facilities and the lifetime changes as a result. For the genealogists and historians, they are reminded how the study of family history is important in our lives. Gwendolyn McMillan Lawe describes how knowing her history has enhanced her appreciation of her rural upbringing and the many individuals that influenced her to become the successful, accomplished individual that she is today. She tells her story from a front row seat.

Harry Robinson, Jr., President and CEO
African American Museum, Dallas, Texas

Introduction

This history was compiled by Gwendolyn McMillan Lawe, daughter of the late A.C. McMillan and Modis McMillan (to whom this history is dedicated), of Emory Texas. I have always felt that if one's history is to be written accurately, one has to take part in the writing of that history.

Over the past several years, I have asked family members to assist me in this endeavor. However, I must say, I have been able to gain little information from family members. Therefore, you will see that there is more information on the A.C. McMillan Family than there is on other families (for obvious reasons). After all, this is "my" story. I have also included family genealogy information in Chapter 4.

Initially, my intent was to compile this history and publish it for other family members. I felt that this would be a worthwhile fundraiser for the A.C. McMillan Scholarship Fund and that family members could purchase copies at the McMillan Reunion. Because of an apparent lack of interest (and because my original draft was lost), the process of writing was slowed down. This simply meant that my efforts were stalled—not stopped. I continually gather information;

and I feel that at the time of this publication, I will still be gathering information—perhaps for another edition.

With the use of modern technology, the computer—and especially the use of the Internet—my task has been made easier; and at the same time it has made this assignment expand beyond what I imagined a few years ago. Initially, I intended to do just a genealogical study of my family. There were several McMillans in the family history that I wanted to know more about; and thanks to the Internet, I have learned a little about them. *The Dallas Morning News* has also been an asset in this endeavor. A very interesting article appeared in a special edition during the State Fair of Texas about the McMillans of Dallas. The article was entitled "The 20th Century: Through the Eyes of Texas." There was also an exhibit at the State Fair, which included information about the McMillans and the publication.[1]

In the summer of 1999, my husband and I took a most unusual summer vacation. We traveled two weeks and over 3500 miles by car. We visited family members and many educational and cultural sites. We visited numerous museums. Among the museums visited was the Smithsonian Institution in Washington, DC. Even though the African Art Museum was one of the highlights of our tour, it was the Beck Cultural Center in Knoxville, Tennessee, which inspired me the most. A very close friend of ours, Avon Rollins, is the Director of the Beck Cultural Center. He gave us a tour of the facility and shared a lot of information about the center and his responsibilities as the director. It was at the Beck Cultural Center that my husband and I decided that we could do something similar to the Beck Center in memory of my father, just as the Beck Center had been established in memory of one of Knoxville's outstanding citizens. Thus, the idea of the "A.C. McMillan African American Museum" was conceived. It was then

1 "The 20th Century: Through the Eyes of Texas," *Dallas Morning News*, Sunday, September 26, 1999, pages 34-36.

that I decided that it was important to complete the family history that I had started several years earlier.

It was our vision that the Museum would be open in the fall of 1999 and that a grand opening would be held before the Year 2000. The Museum would be the first of its kind in Rains County. It would provide an opportunity for family members and the residents of Rains County to appreciate the accomplishments of African Americans both nationally and locally. The essence of the Museum would be to document and record the history of African Americans in the region around Emory, Texas. To accomplish this task would require investigating local African American family trees, studying their institutions (schools, churches, etc.), and reviewing their social and economic circumstances. Many African American families in the Emory area date back over 150 years. In this publication, I have tried to trace the history of the McMillans, as well as other African American families, in Emory (Rains County) from its earliest beginnings. I feel that knowing some of Emory's history is necessary to understand how I got from "Wolf (the community of my birth) to Wolfwood (the name of my street today)."

Chapter 1
Where Is Emory, Texas?

In 1870 by taking off corners of Wood, Van Zandt, Hunt, and Hopkins Counties, Rains County was formed. Emory, the County Seat, received its name from Emory Rains, Republic of Texas leader. Emory Rains was born in Warren County, Tennessee, and moved to Texas in 1817. Emory Rains held many public offices in other Texas counties before coming to Rains County. His life was devoted to that of a public servant. In 1866, Emory Rains rode a mule to Austin, Texas, for the purpose of getting a bill introduced to create Rains County. Rains became a county in 1870.[2]

It is important to point out that there were African Americans in Rains County prior to 1870. Also, it is important to note that an African American, Sol Jackson (my great-grandfather), came to Texas with Emory Rains. At least, that is the way our history has been handed down. The African American community in Emory, Jacksonville, is named after Sol Jackson. There were two other African American communities in Emory—Wolf and Sand Flat.

Pioneer African American families lived in segregated communities,

2   http://rains-tx.tamu.edu/ (accessed January 20, 2007)

1

attended segregated schools, and had their own churches and lodges. These institutions played an important role in the livelihood of the African American families. At the time, for many individuals, the church was the only organization that African Americans could be active members and hold positions of leadership. It was the church that would eventually be the model for other organizations to be formed by African Americans. All community meetings were held at the churches or at the schools.

Chapter 2
The Early Years

On February 3, 1948, I was born in Emory, Texas. I was not born in a hospital; I was delivered by my grandmother (a mid-wife, which was the usual method of birth in the community where I was born at that time). I was the second child to be born to Alfred (A.C.) and Modis McMillan. My brother, Alfred, was almost four years old when I was born.

Growing up in Emory, I am sure, was not too different from growing up in other small East Texas towns. However, I have many fond memories of my childhood. Back then, living in a segregated America was just a way of life. I began school at age six in 1954. Ironically, this was the year of the Supreme Court Decision, Brown v Board of Education. Of course, at age six, I did not understand what this meant (or would mean) in the education of African Americans in America and in Rains County specifically. My father and mother did not let us entertain the thought that we were "second class," even though we might have been treated as such by the whites during this same time period. It wasn't that we did not know that segregation was the "way of the South," we were just sheltered from it as much as possible. Although African Americans could not use public facilities such as restrooms, drink from public fountains, or eat at restaurants that were available to the general public, we just did not allow ourselves to be subjected to such discrimination when we could avoid it. So, whenever possible, we patronized African American establishments. I do remember the passage of the Civil Rights Bill of 1964, which enabled African Americans to use public facilities. However, I don't remember that having an immediate direct effect on my life.

My parents would take the family to Dallas for an evening of entertainment. This usually included eating at a drive-in restaurant such as Good Luck's hamburgers and a movie at the State Theater or the Forest Theater, which were located in the African American parts of town. Since we were not accustomed to eating in restaurants anyway, eating at the Good Luck was something special. At the time, there were many African American movies that were shown at the State and Forest Theaters. There were also concerts that were held at the Sportatorium and the Dallas Convention Center. My father's good friend, A. Q. Randolph, worked at these concerts (I am not sure in what capacity) and he got tickets for us to see such entertainers as Jackie Wilson and Johnny Taylor. These are two that I can remember that I attended with my father as a child. However, sometimes my parents attended these concerts without taking us. I can remember my mother talking about their going out to dinner at The Green Parrot, which was a restaurant and club that featured live entertainment with dinner.

When traveling to distant places such as to visit relatives in such west Texas cities as Amarillo, Borger, El Paso, Wichita Falls, Lubbock, and Electra, we would always travel with food packed for eating along the way. Often, my father would stop at a grocery store, buy cold cuts, bread, etc., and we ate at roadside parks. I guess it never really occurred to me that we could not have eaten in the restaurants (if we had wanted to) or that we could not stay in the motels along the way. It was also a family tradition when I was young to travel to Lawton, Oklahoma for the Easter Pageant, which was an annual event held before daylight Easter Sunday morning. This too was one of the trips that we packed food, traveled at night, and stayed in the car until the pageant occurred before daylight. Once the pageant program ended, we drove back to Emory to spend the rest of Easter Sunday services at Prairie Grove, our church.

Home Training

During my childhood days, it was thought that a child's behavior was governed by the child's "home training." Parents did not wait until their children entered school to learn such things as manners and self-discipline. A child learned such things as "excuse me," "thank you," "yes/no ma'am/sir," and "please" and all were considered a part of home training. Children were taught to be respectful of themselves as well as others and they especially had to be respectful of adults. No child could call an adult by the first name. And just a sharp "yes" or "no" was unacceptable when speaking to adults. Children who did not display such characteristics were said to have had "no home training."

Household Chores

As a young child, I always had chores. The earliest chores that I can remember included mainly washing dishes and helping my mother with the cooking and cleaning. When I was about six, my mother started teaching me to wash the dishes. I was hardly tall enough to reach the cabinet, but using a stool, I was able to wash the dishes. By the way, that stool was a little red stool that read: "This little stool of mine, I use it all the time, to reach the things I couldn't, and lots of things I shouldn't." Later on when I was about 10 or 11, I started being more interested in cooking. At the time, Imperial Sugar Company published a cookbook entitled "My first Cookbook." There were ads for it on the television and on the sugar bag. I ordered this cookbook, which motivated me to begin cooking by recipe—namely, cookies. Although with the help of my mother, I did learn to make simple cakes and cookies by using the recipes, cooking in our house usually did not involve using "written" recipes. Recipes were just handed down from generation to generation and you just remembered how to cook. As I grew older the chores included more cooking and washing and ironing. When I was a child, doing the laundry was a little more than merely washing and drying the clothes. My mother had a washing machine that had a wringer. When the clothes were washed, she would take them from the wash water, run them through the wringer, and into the rinse water. Once rinsed, they would be put through the wringer again and then they would be hung onto the clothesline. Although, I was not fond of hanging the clothes on the line, there was not a better way of having clean, fresh-smelling linens. Of course, it was another story when it came to the clothes. Since "wash and wear" was not the case, most items of clothing had to be ironed. This involved "sprinkling" the clothes first and placing them in a bundle to be ironed later. I can even remember that my mother would sometimes place the clothes in the refrigerator if it were going to be a while before she would finish the ironing. This way she did not have to worry about their turning sour or having mildew. Once the clothes had set for a sufficient amount of time the ironing was much easier. But then there were my dad's khaki pants. I don't think that there was anything that could make them easy to iron. Of all the things that I can remember ironing, khakis were the hardest to iron. They required a little starch, just as most of the clothing did at that time. Sometimes the starching was done as a part of the laundry process and sometimes it was sprayed on. Either way, this was not a step in the laundry process that I was fond of.

Since I was the only female of four siblings, I think that I was expected to do the work that was considered "women's work." However, thanks to my parents, they required all of us to pitch in to keep the house clean, as well as the yard. However, my brothers did most of the yard work. They were really skilled at doing the yard work. Since I did not do the yard work, I did more of the housework than they did. I often cooked for them. They would always tease me about my cooking—especially the cookies—but they always ate them all!

Games Children Played (without toys)

Growing up in Emory in the early 50's was not too different from other places at the time as far as games children played—or was it? Back then, many of the games that we played included using the children's imagination rather than playing with toys. I can remember when spending the night with other children (my cousins), often the games played consisted of playing with each other rather than playing with toys. For example, story-telling was quite popular. I can remember that there was a tale about "Fat Man, Fat Man." There were many others, but that one stands out to me. We would tell the story and, even though I had heard it before, it was always interesting to hear a different person's take on the same story. ("Fat Man, Fat Man, why are you so fat?" "I eat a pan of corn bread; drink a barrel of milk; eat you if I catch you!")

Then, there were games that did not require toys such as "Pop the Whip." In this game, children would hold hands and run. The children at the beginning of the line, which were usually the larger ones, would stop quickly causing the ones on the end to disjoin. If you were not able to hold on, you would be out of the game. There were also games such as "Ring around the Roses." This game was usually played when little girls got together. This game involved holding hands in a circle singing "Ring around the roses; pocket full of posies, sweet milk, buttermilk, last one squat." There was also the game of "London Bridge." In this game, two children would hold their hands together as high as they could reach and the rest of the children would form a line and go underneath the hands ("the bridge") singing "London Bridge is falling down, falling down, falling down; London Bridge is falling down, my fair lady." The child that was caught underneath ("the bridge") at the end of the song would be caught—therefore out of the game. Another game that was popular at the time was "Little Sally Walker." This game was popular with little girls (for obvious reasons—Little Sally Walker). In this game, children would gather in a circle around one child in the center of the circle. The one in the circle would squat as the others sang "Little Sally Walker, sitting in a saucer, rise Sally rise. Put your hands on your hips, and let your backbone slip. Shake it to the east; oh shake it to the west. Shake it to the one that you love best." Then she (the child in the circle) would choose the next child to be in the center of the circle. "Hide and Seek" was often played when children got together and played games. This game did not require many players nor did it require any equipment or toys. Children often jumped rope also. This game was not played with a "jump rope" that was purchased for the purpose of the game. It was usually with a rope that was also used for other reasons. But somehow, children usually found a rope when there were enough children to play. Two children were needed to swing the rope around as a third child stepped in and out and "jumped" the rope. When the children were more skilled several would jump at a time.

Games children played (with toys)

I guess that during my childhood, the most popular toys for

African American children growing up in Emory were very much the same as elsewhere in this country—dolls for little girls and guns for little boys. However, these were toys that children got for Christmas and they usually were only gotten at Christmas. This meant that they did not last all year. At this time, little girls had to accept "white" dolls because there usually were no African American dolls in the stores. (I am not sure if they would have been chosen if they had been in the stores.) African American dolls, when they were found, were not the pretty dolls and they did not wear the beautiful clothes that the white dolls wore. It was like they were designed not to appeal to little girls. Often the hair was painted on and little girls wanted to have dolls that they could comb the hair. Dressing and undressing them was also desirable. At the time, most dolls did nothing, i.e., walk, talk, etc. I can remember after I was a little older and not much interested in dolls that there was a doll called "Betsy Wetsy" which simply meant that she would "wet" after having her bottle and a "Chatty Cathy" which meant that the doll actually talked. The only little girl that I remember having this doll was Betty Jean Woosley. Although I had outgrown playing with dolls, Chatty Cathy was different because it talked. I can remember that her mother, Mrs. Arversia Woosley, would always enjoy showing off this talking doll, and we all marveled at her talking.

For little boys, the popular gun sets were based on the popular western characters on television and in comic books. For example, Roy Rogers, Wild Bill Hickok, the Lone Ranger, or Hop-along-Cassidy were all very popular. Then there were other weapons such as Zorro's sword. The fortunate little boys often were able to get other items such as hats, capes, masks, chaps, or lariats. These items, along with their cap guns, enabled them to really enact the parts of the characters seen on the television. Although the western toys were the most popular for boys, there were other toys such as the military toys. However, probably after playing with guns, young boys preferred playing sports next. These games did not require many items. For example, basketball, baseball, softball, and football were games that did not require much more than one or two items per boy. In our neighborhood, there was a basketball goal, so there were always a few basketballs. Some of the boys had bats, gloves, and balls, so it was always easy to play ball whenever there were enough children to play. Often, if it was basketball, it only meant that there had to be one or two willing to play. Boys played these games most often, but girls often played these games too. (I know that I did.)

Boys also liked playing with cars and trains. Often getting cars and trains were toys that boys received at Christmastime so these toys usually were not played with very much year round—simply because they did not last year round.

Girls and boys also played such games as Jacks and marbles. Although, it is assumed that little girls played Jacks and boys played marbles, I played both. In playing Jacks, a child learned a little about counting because to play you had to know how to count. The game of Jacks involved having the Jacks and a ball. The first player bounced the ball, picked up the jacks, and caught the ball—beginning with picking up one ("the ones") and when all had been picked on one at a time, the player moved on to picking up the "twos," etc. When groups got together at the different homes, there were always Jacks and a ball available—even if they had to be combined to make complete sets. They were always available. Since the ball had to be bounced, and scraping up the Jacks was a part of the game, Jacks had to be played inside the house or on the porch. Although roller skates might have been popular for children in urban areas, games that involved paved sidewalks, driveways, etc. were not popular for obvious reasons.

Playing marbles was somewhat like playing Jacks. Whenever groups of children got together, there were always marbles available. Marbles and Jacks were available in the "Five and Dime" stores year round. Playing marbles was referred to as "shooting marbles." Because of the sand in our community and there being no paved areas, marbles had to be played in the (unpaved) driveways or other areas that were not so sandy in order that the marbles would roll properly. My brother, Jewel (Chief), and cousins, Marcus Garrett, J.W. Garrett, David Garrett, Howard Garrett, Kenneth McMillan, and Fred Hunter were among the marble players usually involved in our neighborhood. The female cousins that usually played with us were Vannie Robinson and Eleanor Davis. Fannie Garrett and Jacqueline "Jackie" Wright were around, but they were a little young. When staying at my grandmother, Mama Lucy's house, Larry Robinson and Patricia "Sue" Hobbs also played with us. And, by the way, playing outside often included chewing some "sour dock," which I have never seen or heard of since my childhood.

As boys grew older, they often became more interested in sports and spent little time playing with toys. Girls, too, only played with dolls when they were small. However, playing ball or playing Jacks and marbles were popular games even into the teens.

Toys that were often made by children

As a little girl, soft drink bottles were often used to make what we called "rope dolls." As I mentioned earlier, girls liked combing the hair on their dolls and most often the only dolls that they had were "blondes." During this time period, ice could be bought in what was called "by the block." It was wrapped in rope. (I guess this was to enable one to pick up the ice.) This rope was a blondish color. Thus, this rope was perfect for the hair of the rope doll. In order to make a doll, all you needed to do was cut the rope and insert it into the top of the bottle until in was secured tightly enough that you could comb the hair. Often these bottles were "Coke" bottles, but any kind of bottle could be used. Usually, these dolls would not be dressed. It was the hair that determined the looks of the doll. We would braid (plait) the hair, curl the hair, wash the hair, and often tie ribbons on the hair. I actually remember more about rope dolls than I can remember any particular doll that I owned as a child.

Little boys, when playing outside, often made guns out of sticks. They would chase each other pretending to be shooting the sticks. They also made bows and arrows. The bows were made from small trimmed limbs from trees that were green and would bend into the bow. Then, twine was used to tie on each end. The arrows were sticks. They also would use items such as matchboxes or any other small boxes for cars. When playing in the sand, pushing small boxes (or bottles) in the sand would make a road and almost any push item could be improvised for a car. Also, after rain and the sand was slightly moist, children would play cars and use their hands and feet in the sand to make houses. In placing the feet underneath sand packed on top, this would make a garage onto the house.

Playground Equipment

As a child in a small town, there were no parks or recreation facilities for African Americans. In Emory, the only playground that children had was the playground at school (Sand Flat). There we had a seesaw, swings, and a merry-go-round. There was also a swing (that still stands) that consisted of a tall pole with single chains hanging from the top with a handle for gripping at the end of the chains. In order to swing, the child run would around the pole in a circle and lift the feet from the ground to swing around the pole. I described this swing because it was not the typical swing that was usually a part of playground equipment. There was no slide, even though slides were a popular part of playground equipment at that time.

There was an unpaved basketball court with goals at each end. I guess that you could say that this basketball court was somewhat of a community basketball court. This basketball court was also the venue for the basketball games between other schools. It was outside and not fenced in so the neighborhood children always had the basketball court, as well as the other playground equipment, at their disposal.

Baseball and softball areas were also a part of the playground. Other than bats, balls, and bases, these games did not require much equipment. These areas also were available at all times and the sites for games that were played between Sand Flat and other schools. Although students at Sand Flat School ran track, there never was an actual "track" on the campus. However, I do remember that there were shot puts available for those that trained for the shot put in competition. I don't remember that being anything that anyone else did as a pastime.

City Park

For as long as I can remember, the City of Emory has always had a City Park. However, as a child, this was not a place that I ever went. The playground equipment there was always sparse; but there was a tennis court and a basketball court. This was probably the first tennis court that I had ever seen and because of segregated public accommodations, I only "saw" it.

No Kindergarten!

Back in the 50's before I started to school, formal education for African Americans, as well as for Whites in Emory, started with the first grade. I can remember that I was so anxious to begin school. In fact, I thought that since my father was the principal, I should be able to start at five instead of six. However, he felt differently. I can remember that back in those days, students were allowed to pray in school, and I learned the Lord's Prayer and the Pledge of Allegiance. This was part of my readiness for beginning first grade.

At this time, the school and the church were the centers of all social activities. Therefore, children were anxious to attend both. I can remember that at school we had all kinds of things to keep us entertained. Even some of the learning activities were entertaining.

Mrs. Doris Robinson (Washington) was my primary teacher. In the primary grades you learned the basics—The Three R's—"Reading, 'Riting and 'Rithmetic." I cannot remember a lot about the books that we read except lines like "Look. Look. See Spot run." But I do remember how much fun it was to have spelling class when you would line up and spell until the last person was left not missing a word in the spelling list. I guess that this was the equivalent of having spelling bees. We just called it spelling. And the timetables were fun too. Not only did we have to know how to multiply (on paper) but we had to say the timetables aloud. Now students (and adults) are so dependent upon the computer and calculators, they could not begin to say the 2, 3, 4, 5-timetables aloud. And then there was learning to write cursive. I could hardly wait to learn to write in cursive. Mrs. Robinson was a very good teacher. She expected (demanded) the best from us and that is what she got.

In the intermediate grades, I had Mrs. Terecia V. Maples (Caraway) and Mrs. Bonnie Willie Williams as teachers. Both were very good teachers, but I cannot remember a lot of outstanding events associated with their classes except that Mrs. Maples was a very good musician (and singer). She played piano for the church and she also played for the programs at school. I can remember that she had two children that were about the same age as my brother Jewel and me. They lived with Mr. and Mrs. Gordie Garrett for a while and then they lived in a mobile home. Her daughter, Valeria, and I became good friends. I even spent weekends with them when they would go home to Henderson, Texas. Mrs. Bonnie Williams was the wife of my father's good friend, Mr. Cleveland Williams. In fact, both of my parents were close friends with Mr. and Mrs. Williams. My brother, Jewel "Chief" was in their wedding. I think that my father was the best man, but I was a little young to remember details.

Then came the junior high grades when my father was my teacher and principal. My father was an outstanding math and social studies teacher. I always made good grades, but these were by no means favorite classes for me. However, there were some fun activities like my father having us do the "Chicken" as we did the timetables. This was a popular dance at the time. He thought that it would be a good idea to do the timetables as we did the Chicken. Of course, most of the girls enjoyed doing this. However, I can remember that one of my cousins, Lee Hobbs, had a tough time concentrating on the timetables as he did the Chicken. My friend, Anna Dean Miles, who was always tickled at something, had a tough time maintaining her composure and we all got very serious cases of the giggles. Another time that I can remember getting in trouble because of our laughing was when we were sitting in class and Mr. Jack Briscoe passed by on a horse and Anna Dean got tickled. Of course, her getting tickled set us all off.

An interesting thing about going to Sand Flat was that my father was the principal. He was the uncle or cousin of most of the other students that attended while I was there. The Hunters and the Porters were about the only ones that were not related to us. However, most of the students called him "Uncle A.C."

Back during those days, some of the favorite activities of students at Sand Flat included participating in the Interscholastic League.

15

At that time we simply referred to it as "The League." This allowed students to participate in literary contests such as spelling, speaking, singing, and playing the piano. I can remember that I competed in the oratorical contests. I can remember reciting the poem "Oh Captain, My Captain." I competed more than once, but that is the poem that I remember. I can remember Dianne McMillan (Crowe) competing against Beverly Rector (Hunter) in the singing category. At that time, Beverly lived in Caddo Mills. After marrying Fred Hunter, she later moved to Emory. There were also the track and field events. During this time, Sand Flat had students that participated in all of the above. The women teachers coached the students in the literary events and my father, the principal, coached all of the track and field events.

Participation in the Interscholastic League gave Sand Flat students an opportunity to compete against students from the nearby surrounding towns. Often, winners would go on to compete at the state meetings, which would be held at Prairie View. I don't know if we ever had state winners, but I do know that we did have those to compete at the state meet. I can remember that Edwin Collins was a track star at Sand Flat. However, this was before my time at Sand Flat. But I do remember that my father took him to Prairie View to compete in the state meet. There were also several of the Hunter children that were very outstanding in sports.

Other extracurricular activities included our having basketball teams that competed with the schools in the surrounding communities. I can remember especially playing against Dunbar (Lone Oak) and Caddo Mills. Perhaps I remember these schools because of the relationships that my father had with the teachers and administrators at these schools. Mrs. Olivia Scales was the principal at Lone Oak and Mr. Clyde Simmons was the principal in Caddo Mills. I even remember that once Lone Oak needed players to play on their team in a tournament and our girls' basketball team played for their team.

There was always a special bond between the students from the Sand Flat, Richland, and Lone Oak communities. We all knew each other because of school and because of church. Our churches all fellowshipped with each other so it seemed only natural that we would participate in school activities together, too. In fact, when I graduated from Sand Flat, it was a joint commencement with Sand Flat and Richland eighth graders combined. There were a total of nine of us and the ceremony was held at Prairie Grove Baptist Church in Emory. We did not wear caps and gowns. We wore navy blue skirts and slacks and white blouses and shirts. This was a very exciting time in our lives because this meant that we would now graduate and go on to high school at St. Paul High School in Greenville. Yes, we were really excited about the 40-mile one-way trip that we would now be making as a part of our daily routine. We were so anxious to graduate from elementary school and go to high school that we had no idea what the conditions would be.

Picture of Sand Flat School building taken in 2005

The Summer School

One of the things that I can remember about attending Sand Flat School is that we would get out for the summer just as schools do today. However, we would go back later on in the summer (I think July) in order that we could be out during the fall for cotton-picking season. This is a part of my past that I think that I try not to remember, but it is a part of my past. The technique was not picking cotton (which means picking the cotton from the bowl), but it was actually pulling cotton.

Because my father had always been a professional person with a job as principal and always had other part-time jobs, I don't think that the family income depended upon the children of my family picking cotton. However, my father was the type of person that felt that his children were no exception. If school was to turn out for picking cotton, then we were to pick cotton too.

I can remember that we rode in the backs of trucks, grown ups and children too. Small children were given what were called tow sacks or croaker sacks. These were about the equivalent of a king-size pillowcase. Older children and adults had cotton sacks, which were made of "ducking" cloth, sometimes called unbleached domestic. I am not sure what that fabric would be called today. These sacks were bought already made. The straps that fit across the shoulder had to be adjusted to fit the individual. Often men would have very long sacks. I never really mastered the art of picking cotton. But I was there in the fields just the same. The weather was often very hot and we would take water breaks by going to the scales, which would be on the trailers where the cotton was taken when one's sack needed to be emptied. Water was usually in a cooler, but there was only one cup or dipper that everyone drank from. No one really worried about hygiene when it came to drinking the cool water. We were not aware of contracting diseases in this way.

There were long rows of cotton. The cotton picker would walk between the rows and pick cotton from the rows on each side. Children would usually pick from only one row, but adults would pick from two rows. Sometimes two people would share a middle row. This was called "snatching a row." If the cotton was really thick, and the rows were really long, it could possibly take all day to get to the end of the rows. When lunchtime came, usually the cotton pickers would all go to a shaded area and eat the lunches that they had brought with them. The cotton owner usually furnished cool water. Sometimes these lunches would include such things as cold cut sandwiches, cold cuts and crackers, or crackers and Vienna sausage, deviled ham, or potted meat. Of these, I only liked the cold cut sandwiches. Often there was

Kool-Aid or tea, depending on whether there was ice. And sometimes the tea or Kool-aid was brought from home in a thermos with ice. Once lunch was eaten, there was not much time wasted before going back and finding where you had left your sack, or where you left off. Sometimes the sack was used as your seat while eating lunch.

It was common for men to pick over 200 pounds of cotton per day. I usually picked near 100. However, there were some young girls and women who picked over 200 pounds too. I can remember that my father would threaten me by saying that if I did not pick 100 pounds, I should bring a switch when I came home. I actually remember bringing a switch and letting it fall from the truck on the way home. I don't remember what happened after I lost the switch!

I am not sure how many weeks were spent during the fall picking cotton, but I am sure that I was always glad to see those weeks pass and to be able to get back to school. It's hard to imagine that anyone was really able to profit financially from picking cotton, other than the owner of the cotton fields. I cannot remember the exact amount paid, but I think that the pay was about two cents per pound. This meant that if I picked 100 pounds of cotton, I only earned two dollars ($2) for working all day in the hot sun. At the end of a week, I would have earned about $10.

Church Activities

Just as in most of the families in the community, going to church was a big part of our lives. Sunday services included going to Sunday school, morning service, Baptist Training Union (BTU), and night service. Sometimes, an afternoon service would be held also. This was when we would fellowship with neighboring churches—Richland, Lone Oak, Sulphur Springs, etc. Although I really liked attending church at that time, I did not get much pleasure from attending B.T.U. I can remember telling my mother "When I grow up, no one will ever have to tell me to go to church—I will. But I won't go to B.T.U." Once I grew up and moved away from home, my new church did not have B.T.U.

Another thing that was somewhat unusual about Prairie Grove back in the days of my youth (although, at the time, it was not unusual at all) was that the church only had regular Sunday services twice a month. In those days, Prairie Grove had a full day of church services on the first and third Sundays. Richland, on the other hand, had services on the second and fourth Sundays. So on the Sundays that the regular church services were not held, there would only be Sunday school in the mornings and BTU in the evenings. However, as I grew older, Prairie Grove was able to become a full-time church—having services on every Sunday of the month. This was when Reverend Cleveland Alexander was the pastor. Because we (Prairie Grove) were members of the Cypress Association of Churches, we participated in what was called "Fifth Sunday Board Meeting." At these meetings, all of the churches in the district participated in services and meetings on the weekend of the Fifth Sunday. On Sunday mornings, after attending Sunday school at our own church, often we would attend the Board Meeting services (11:00 a.m. service) at the member church that hosted the meeting. These Fifth Sunday Board meetings have been continuous for many years.

At that time, there were a lot of children in my age group attending Prairie Grove. We had Sunday school classes for all age groups and we had choirs for different age groups. Also at this time, the musicians were often teachers at Sand Flat or my cousins Bobbie Davis (Cox), Emma McMillan (Madlock), and Patricia Jackson. I can remember that some of the Sunday school teachers were Mrs. Furiel Johnson and Mrs. Aline Randolph. Of course there were others, but these are the ones that stand out to me as being my Sunday school teachers when I was growing up in Emory. These were also the individuals involved in the planning of the programs at church on the various holidays such as Christmas, Mother's Day, and Easter. Later on Aunt Florene McMillan and Aunt Claressa McMillan became youth leaders. However, this was after I was no longer a youth at Prairie Grove.

Going to church afforded us much more than just a religious education. It was truly a social outlet as well. My cousin, Fannie Garrett (Brown), and I were first cousins and we were also close friends. She and I both started taking music lessons from Mrs. A. J. Lewis in Lone Oak when we were quite young. Looking back on this, I think that Mrs. Lewis was truly a pioneer in teaching music. Each Saturday morning she would teach music to a group of African American girls in her living room in Lone Oak. I am sure that she probably received all kinds of criticism for doing this. However, it was from Mrs. Lewis that Fannie and I were first taught to play the piano. There were a number of others before us and a few after us; but Fannie and I went on to become the musicians for the Prairie Grove Church for several years. Actually, Fannie was much more gifted in playing the piano. She had what people called "an ear" for music. I simply read the music and played it—not much variation from the written music.

Being the musicians for the church meant that we often had to travel with the pastor, Reverend Cleveland Alexander, and the choir when they would visit other churches throughout the area. As the musicians and as dependable youth members of the church, we were often chosen to represent the church at the annual Sunday school and B.T.U. Congress. This was an annual conference held each summer at the various churches throughout the Cypress District, which included Prairie Grove. Since this was a time when African Americans did not stay in hotels and were not allowed to eat in restaurants, young people would attend the conference and would stay in the homes of church members during the period that they attended the Congress. Fannie and I stayed in such places as Mt. Pleasant, Naples, and Sulphur Springs. There were also times when young people from other cities stayed in our homes when the Congress met at Prairie Grove. For Fannie and me, these were excellent times to meet youth from other churches—especially the young men! We even had boyfriends that we only saw at these meetings. At the time, neither Fannie nor I was actually dating. But we did have boyfriends at these meetings. I must also mention that we did get paid for playing piano for the church--$5 per Sunday. That meant $2.50 each. We decided between ourselves that we would get $5 every other Sunday rather than receive $2.50 each Sunday. That way it seemed like a little more money.

The Role of the Church and the Cypress Association

In 1860, on the Teal Plantation, a young male preacher by the name of Cicero Commodore Chambers was determined to be free. He worked overtime for his master in order to be free. He had been brought from Virginia to Texas in 1856. He bought a young woman for $1,500 (a large amount of money for the time). This process was slow, so he sold her to a nearby plantation with the understanding that he would redeem her at a later date, which he did. This young preacher served as the leader, or Moderator, of the Cypress District Association from 1873-1895.

The Reverend A. D. Sanders in his book entitled *A Factual History of Cypress District Baptist Association, 1872 - 1973*, describes how a 10-county area (Kaufman, Hunt, Rains, Wood, Upshur, Hopkins, Franklin, Camp, Titus, and Morris) came together emerging from the shackles of slavery, unskilled and illiterate. However, through cooperation and hard labor, the Church was the Negroes' medium of "mass communication." In 1873, "a group of ordinary people met in the Ripley Creek Baptist Church of Mt. Vernon, Texas. They were not too far removed from the black night of slavery and the dust or affliction had not wholly lifted from their longing path. They would not be mastered by a negative past, neither would they be dominated by the social, political, and economic injustices of their time. Possessed with the spirit of Christ, they applied the Christian religion, with Jesus as the norm, to the perplexing problems of their day."

Cypress' Objectives

These noble souls organized Cypress District Baptist Association. By doing so, they set in motion a movement for God and the advancement of His Kingdom and for the advancement of its people. Among the objectives of this association were:

- To promote an evangelical ministry throughout the District, State and Nation;
- To promote Christian Education;
- To maintain a unified home life;
- To encourage people to regularly support Christian Education; and
- To achieve first-class citizenship.

In order to insure that respect be given to all individuals, it was a written rule that all be addressed as "Brother" or "Sister, or by their titles such as Moderator, Dean, etc.

Scholarship Investments

From its beginning, Cypress gave support to higher education. In 1881, F. I. S. College at Wolf City, Texas was the first educational institution supported by Cypress Baptist Association. Later its support was given to Bishop College, Marshall, Texas and Dallas, Texas. The scholarship fund was established in 1944 to send worthy students to Bishop College. Several students from Rains County received scholarships from Cypress. Others received different scholarships and financial aid to attend Bishop College.

Some Personalities of Cypress District

Dr. D. Edwin Johnson, of Point, Texas, pastored several churches throughout Texas and later became the Director of Southern Baptist Institute in Dallas. Dr. T. M. Chambers, son of Cypress' founder, Rev. Cicero C. Chambers, pastored in Texas, Arkansas, and California. He was the founder and President of the Progressive National Baptist Convention, U.S.A. Dr. L. B. Moss, a native of Greenville, Texas, was a pastor for one year in Cypress and later founded the California State Baptist Convention. Professor C. C. Wesley (Principal of the Richland School) served as the third Dean of Cypress.

In 1889, the Cypress Association pooled its finances to help liberate Negro farmers and their families. Through the guidance of F.I.S. College, their monies were matched with Farmers Improved Society funds to assist farmers who had been denied loans from many banks in East Texas. Also, in 1889, the Women's Convention of Cypress was organized. During the third administration, with Naomi C. Hill, serving as president, Mrs. Olivia G. Scales (who died recently) was elected treasurer. Also, Furilee Johnson, Modean Lane, Florene McMillan, Modis McMillan, and Gletha Davis were among members from Emory who were active in the Women's Convention. Mrs. Lillie V. Sanders, wife of the pastor of Richland Baptist Church, served as one of the vice presidents during the 1945-1973 administration.

In 1961, the workers of Cypress Sunday School and Baptist Training Union Congress were inspired through Dr. Melvin J. Banks of Bishop College to teach and train Baptist in every local church. Dr. Banks emphasized the importance of good leadership and that leaders become community minded. In 1961, when the Congress met in Emory at the Prairie Grove Baptist Church, Dr. Banks was houseguest of the A. C. McMillan family. Fannon Garrett, of Prairie Grove, is seen in the forefront in the picture below at the 1961 Cypress Meeting at Prairie Grove Baptist Church.

The Hopewell Church was organized in 1865 in Emory. This church is no longer in existence. It was discontinued in or about 1912. The Prairie Grove Baptist Church was organized in 1879. One of its early pastors was the Reverend C. C. Chambers. Listed as outstanding personalities from the Prairie Grove Baptist Church from Emory were: J. L. Robinson, Johnnie Snell, A. C. McMillan, Alex Ivey, Gordie Garrett, A. W. Nash, Aubrey Johnson, and David Garrett. Outstanding personalities from Richland Baptist Church (organized in 1876) in Point were: Revs. A. D. Greer, Ivory, S. J. Greer, Dr. D.

Edwin Johnson, and Emmit Greer, Seamore Edwards, Ike Hawkins, Prof. C. C. Wesley and Mrs. Omae Wesley.[3]

Cypress Today

Today, annual summer meetings of the Cypress District Association are called the Congress. These meetings of the Association rotate to the churches throughout the District. Quarterly Board Meetings are held on the weekend of the fifth Sunday also on a rotating basis. Some of the early meetings of the Cypress Association at Prairie Grove in Emory include the 1895 meeting and in 1901 the meeting was held at the Richland Baptist Church in Point, Texas. Prairie Grove Baptist Church in Emory and the Richland Baptist Church remain active members of these meetings, according to long-time Cypress member, Modean Lane, of the Prairie Grove Baptist Church. She has fond memories of her attending these meetings throughout the years.[4]

The Neighborhoods

There is a popular African proverb "It takes a village to raise a child." Back when I was growing up in Emory, it really did "take a village." In fact, the neighborhood (or village) was actually made up of my relatives. I was born on what is now "McMillan Street." Back then, my Grandfather, Jewel McMillan, lived next door to us. His wife, Elberta, was referred to as Nanaw (not Nana) by most of the children in the community, even if she was not their grandmother. He was called "Daddy Jewel" by all of his grandchildren and most of the children in the community also. I remember only a few children referring to him as "Mr. Jewel." This small house is where my parents and my two older brothers and I lived until after I had started to

---

3 Rev. A. D. Sanders, *A Factual History of Cypress District Baptist Association, Sept. 1872-1973*, Self- Published, 1973.
4 Discussion with Modean Lane at A. C. McMillan Museum on February 4, 2007 (her 85th birthday).

school. Although this was a very small house, it was at this house that we had one of the first television sets in the community. Our living room would be filled with children and adults on Sunday evening to watch television. Lassie and Rin Tin Tin are two of the earliest television programs that I can remember watching. There were not a lot of other programs at that time. It is hard to imagine that our small living room held about 20 people.

Next door to us, on the opposite side of my grandfather's house, was another small house. At one time, my mother's brother, Uncle Choycie Robinson and his wife Doris (who would later become Mrs. Doris Washington) lived next door to us. Later on Peal and Betty (Boyd) Jackson lived in the same little house. They had two children—Jeletha (daughter) and Larry when they lived there.

A little down the road from our house across the road was the home of Cutis Thomas and his wife Neet. (I am sure that was not her given name, but that is what she was called.) Next to their house was my father's sister, Aunt Mildred (Garrett). Aunt Mildred and her husband, Uncle Dave, had five sons—Hobert, David, Howard, Delenis, and Thomas (Tony). David was the one that was my age. Aunt Mildred and Uncle Dave also were among the first in the community to have a television set. I can remember that Aunt Mildred would put the television in the window facing outward and lots of children would come to her house to watch cartoons—much like being at a movie.

Across the road from where Aunt Mildred lived was Mrs. Willie Phillips. Mrs. Willie (as we called her) owned a pear orchard that was next to the road. I can remember that was when I learned the word "orchard." Her daughter, Mrs. Zula Cullors, lived with her. I guess that she had some type of mental illness. I can remember that she was always very nice, but I can remember that I was always somewhat afraid of her because I could not understand her when she would be talking sometime. I think that at the time I was told that she had experienced a "nervous breakdown." This term was new and vague to me. She had a son whose name was Alton Cullors who lived in California. Alton and his wife had a large family. They would come to Texas each summer and they would travel in a pickup with a camper. This was the first time I had known anyone with a camper and the first time that I had been able to actually see the inside of it. This was truly a spectacular vehicle. Alton and his wife had one daughter, Celeste. I don't remember her age, but I can remember that she was younger than me. I would always visit her and she visited me on a few occasions. I usually would visit Mrs. Willie often when Alton and his family would be there.

Later, we moved into a larger home, which is where we were living when my youngest brother, Harold, was born. By the way, he was the first of my siblings to be born in a hospital. The other three of us had been delivered by midwife. (Actually, I think that the midwife was my maternal grandmother, Mama Lucy Robinson.) Before moving to this larger house, we had not enjoyed such conveniences (or luxuries) as indoor plumbing and telephones that did not have party lines. At that time, a party line meant that when you talked on the phone, it was very much like talking on a phone with others having extensions at their own home (instead of in the next room) and being able to listen to your conversations. This also meant that you could not make a call or receive a call if someone on your line was talking. However, at this time we did actually dial the phone. On the earlier phones, one had to tell the operator the number that you wished to dial.

Moving into this house meant having new next-door neighbors. However, they were just a different set of relatives. To the right was my father's sister, Aunt Modean Lane. To the left was his sister, Aunt Deora Garrett. Aunt Deora and my mother were sisters-in-law and they were very close friends. Aunt Deora was probably the most neighborly of the entire neighborhood. She watched out for the entire neighborhood; she always had her children and some of the other children in the neighborhood, and she often cooked for the neighborhood. She enjoyed keeping children and cooking (at least, that was the impression that I got). Having cooked in many restaurants, she was a first-class cook. It seemed that she knew how to cook everything. Next to Aunt Deora was my mother's sister, Aunt Gletha Davis. Aunt Gletha had three daughters. All of these aunts had children that were close in age to someone in our family. For example, one of Aunt Modean's daughters, Tredis, was the same age as Alfred, my brother. Aunt Deora's son, Marcus, was my age, and Aunt Gletha's daughter, Eleanor, was a year older than me. Her daughters, Bonnie and Bobbie were about the same age as my brother, Alfred. Aunt Deora's daughter, Fannie, was four years younger than me, but because they were next door and she and I were both the only girls in our families, we became very close. Because we became so close and Fannie was always tall for her age, many people thought that we were closer in age. Another cousin, Vannie Robinson (Miles), and I were also close friends. Vannie was the daughter of my father's oldest sister, Irene Robinson. Everyone called her "Cook" or "Cooksie." She was married to Hubert Robinson. We called him "Uncle Stu." He was the only African American butcher in Emory. At that time, there was a meat packing facility in Emory. We called it the locker plant. And that is where Uncle Stu worked. Both of the houses that I lived in when growing up in Emory were in the Wolf community. Wolf was the African American community located nearest to the downtown. I am not sure why it was called Wolf, unless it was a place where wolves had lived. That is a good possibility.

During this time, my grandmother, Mama Lucy, lived in the Sand Flat community. She lived near the church. Next door to Mama Lucy were my mother's brother, Uncle Lonnie Robinson, and his wife, Aunt Matt (Mattie). I always enjoyed spending time at Mama Lucy's because Uncle Lonnie had a big family and there was always something going on at their house. Their son, Larry, and I were the same age and were in the same class throughout elementary and high school. However, at that time, their daughter, Doris, was very fond of me (and I was probably more fond of her) and she enjoyed letting me spend time with her. I can remember that she was in high school at St. Paul when I was very young. She would always talk about taking me to school with her. I don't think that she ever did, but I got so excited just thinking about her doing so. Another thing about Uncle Lonnie's house was that they had a black walnut tree and hickory nut trees. Cracking walnuts and hickory nuts was one of the hardest tasks that one could do in order to be able to get such small amount of nuts. The shells were very hard, and the actual nut was so hard to get out. But I can remember that these were delicious nuts and Uncle Lonnie's property was the only place that I can remember getting them. During this time, my grandmother had a wood heater. I can remember when I was very young hearing her tell the older children to go to Uncle Lonnie's to get some "chips." Not knowing what she meant, I thought that she was talking about potato chips. I went along with them to find out the "chips" meant small chips of wood to put in the wood stove. I was so disappointed! Unlike the black walnuts and hickory nuts (rare), black berries and plums were also found all along the road (not highway) from where we lived to where my grandmother lived. In the spring, both were plentiful, although I was always afraid of snakes, and that was something that one had to look out for when picking berries and plums. At that time, few young people drove and many of the older people did not have cars, so it was not uncommon to walk to my grandmother's house (even though it was about two miles away).

The other community that I have not mentioned is the Jacksonville Community. My father's grandfather, Sol Jackson, had settled in this community when he came to Emory (supposedly with Emory's founder, Emory Rains). This community was made up largely of Jacksons. As a child, I spent lots of time in Jacksonville visiting with my father's Aunt Nellie (Snell), sister to my father's mother, Callie Jackson McMillan. Aunt Nellie attended church at Prairie Grove and on Sundays I can remember going to her house after church. R.P. and Lutishie Smith also lived in Jacksonville. Their daughter, Jannie, and I were very good friends while in elementary school. We were the same age and in the same grade. I can remember when we were actually the same age, weight, and height. It was always fun spending the night with Jannie. Her mother was an excellent cook and it was always fun because of the large number of children. I had never spent the night with so many children before. Also, from the time that I was in the second grade, Anna Dean Miles was my very close friend. She, too, lived in Jacksonville and I often visited her—sometimes spending the night. Her Mother, Mrs. Margaret Miles was also a good cook. I can remember that whenever I spent the night my favorite meal there was pinto beans with ground meat and a layer cake with a light glaze or icing. I guess that it was a caramel cake. Even though I cannot remember what it was called, I still can remember how delicious it was.

I guess that the other thing that stood out about the Jacksonville community is that this was the location of the other African American Church in Emory. At the time, we called it the "Holiness" Church. I think that the appropriate denomination was The Church of God in Christ. Most of the Jacksonville community attended this church and most of the African Americans from the Sand Flat and Wolf Communities attended Prairie Grove Baptist Church. I really did not know anything about denominations; I just knew that I went to the only church in the community (which happened to be Baptist).

Discipline

During my youth, discipline was a responsibility of all adults in the community. I say this because all adults were viewed that way by children. Because of this, a certain amount of respect was always given to adults—simply because they were "adults."

Although very few young people used profanity, it would never be used around adults—nor would any other terms that might have been interpreted as disrespectful.

If children were away from home (my brothers and I included), behavior reflected that learned at home. Any adult observing otherwise immediately reported that behavior to the parents. Since this was a time when most households did not have telephones, it was amazing that news could travel so fast! Often so fast that it made it home before the child!

The Look

When attending church services (or other meetings), there were certain "no-nos." These included excessive talking, gum chewing, eating candy, and writing notes. There were always ushers, as well as other adults to see that we behaved properly. However, during those times that we tested our limits, we would get "the look" from our parents. Once we acknowledged "the look," that was usually enough for our actions to be corrected. Since my father usually sat near the back of the church, it was merely a clearing of the throat as a reminder of his presence. Some children were often disciplined by many of the adults—especially if their parents were not present. However, my parents were almost always present.

Discipline at Home

I grew up in a community and a household where strict discipline was the norm. Probably because of my father's being the principal, discipline in our house was stricter than normal. All of my "coming" and "goings" were strictly monitored. When I started high school, I thought that it would mean new freedom—added privileges. It did not! As a pre-teen, I looked forward to the time that I could dress (and wear my hair) as I pleased. It did not! I especially looked forward to this time because I would be able to date. It did not! Somehow, my father thought that dating should come after age 21. He would tell the students this teasingly. However, as I grew older, I began to think that maybe he really did; and 21 was so many years away.

Corporal Punishment

In school, as well as in our homes, corporal punishment was the "method of choice" for correcting children's behavior. Although there are many theories and schools of thought, corporal punishment seemed to work. Young people were seldom disciplined for repeating the same inappropriate acts. And to my knowledge, none received injuries that made them feel abused or unloved. This was simply a way of correcting inappropriate behavior—and it worked!

Sex Education

During the 1950's and 1960's, sex education was for the most part nonexistent. Basically, you got bits and pieces of information from friends, or older siblings. Occasionally, you might even read something pertaining to sex education. But mostly it was that girls were admonished to "keep your legs closed," "keep your dress down," and "don't get pregnant." Often the word pregnant was not used—instead the term "PG" was used. Also, on those occasions when a girl would become pregnant, it was not glorified. In fact, she could not attend school pregnant; thus, her education usually ended at this stage. This general attitude and the fact that public education would end, probably served as a deterrent to pregnancy as much as having a "sex education class."

Once graduating from Sand Flat and moving on to St. Paul High School many things changed. The conditions at St. Paul were so bad—deplorable—that the school should have been condemned long before I went there. My guess is, attending St. Paul in 1962 when I did, was probably comparable to attending Rains in the early 1900's. For example, the building was in such a state of disrepair that it was not safe. If there were inspections in those days, I am sure that it would have been issued all kinds of safety violations and permanently closed. There were holes in the floors, ceilings, and walls. During rainy days, there were leaks; during cold weather, the wood heaters sometimes did not provide sufficient heat. However, I do think there were gas heaters too. But the wood heaters were the warmest. Often the classrooms were so cold that no teaching (or learning) could take place. We often were allowed to leave the classrooms to go to a warmer area. That usually meant one of two options: (1) Mrs. Thrash's homemaking building or (2) Mr. Cleveland Williams' shop. Both of these areas always seemed to be warm. I think that the homemaking area was a newer more insolated building and the shop had the large wood heaters. Most students that were in classrooms that were not sufficiently warm would be given permission to go to one of these locations. However, I often had a third option—the office. Dating back to when I was at Sand Flat, I had learned to type. My father always had a typewriter in his office. He wanted me to learn to type and Mrs. Robinson taught me to type on that "manual" typewriter. She taught me the basics and with practice I learned to type quite well. So when I was in high school, there would often be typing that needed to be done in the office and I was one of the individuals called upon to do it. At one time, Mrs. Mattie Vaughn was the school secretary. She would have me help her in the office when she needed extra help. I got to know Mrs. Vaughn personally because she and her husband lived in Emory. They had moved from Livingston, Texas to work at St. Paul. He was a teacher and he drove the bus from Emory for a while. I can remember sitting on the seat with Mrs. Vaughn while riding the bus to St. Paul. She talked to the students a lot and always seemed genuinely interested in us.

The Bus Ride

Riding the bus to St. Paul was one of the joys of going to St. Paul. Because of the fun that we had on the bus, and because it was a way of life, we never really thought of it as being tiring or boring. We knew that the bus came about 7:00 – 7:15 a.m. and that we were to be on it when it came. We had to walk to the bus stop. I can remember that my mother would sometimes take me to meet the bus, maybe because of the weather or because I was late. I can also remember that we had such a desire to be at school every day that we were determined not to miss the bus. And on those rare occasions when I did, I can remember my mother taking me to catch up with the bus. Also, I can remember that during my ninth and tenth grade years I had lots of dental work done. Again, in order to not miss school, my mother would take me to the dentist in Greenville and then take me on to school afterwards. During those three years at St. Paul, I probably did not miss over a few days total. I had perfect attendance at least once—maybe more.

Catching the bus was only the first part of the ordeal. The bus had a very long route to be covered before reaching St. Paul in the Neylandville Community. We would board the bus in Emory. From Emory we would go through the Sand Flat and Jacksonville Communities (picking up students along the way) and then go on to the Richland Community in Point. In Point, my best friends Hella Mayberry and Lois Hoskins (Lane), among others would get on the bus. From Point, we went on to Lone Oak. We picked up students near the downtown area and then went out in a rural community called "The Nation." It was in Lone Oak that we picked up one of my classmates and good friends, Ruby K. Brown. From Lone Oak, we went through Cumby to Campbell, where we picked up one student, Larry Price. Larry was the son of my father's cousin, Etta (Doll) Price. This school bus route changed sometimes, according to the drivers and to the students. But it was always a long ride by anyone's standards. However, this long ride enabled us to establish friendships with those that made the daily journey that we may not have established otherwise. The arrival time for us to get to school was somewhere around 8:30 – 9:00 a.m. This often varied for a number of reasons—weather, bus problems, or just being late. Because there were many other students arriving from communities like Sand Flat and Richland, there were other buses arriving at various times also. Often there would be mechanical problems with a bus, and it was not uncommon to reach school just in time to go to lunch. This was because if there was a mechanical problem, our driver would have to wait for another driver to bring a bus after returning from his route. Because often the driver would have to leave us on the bus while he walked to the nearest telephone, which often was not near. There was never any mention of the safety of the students because the driver had to leave for assistance. I guess we just knew that we had to be good and wait until help arrived. Because the bus could break down in inclement weather, we were often left on a cold or a very hot bus.

The bus ride home was always somewhat different. In the mornings, students are a little more sedated. However, it was always more fun in the evenings. Most of the drivers let us off the bus in Lone Oak while he made that part of the route out in "The Nation." This allowed us to have a refreshment break. I can remember that we often got potato chips or Fritos. (I think that they were the only two choices at the time.) Or we would have soft drinks or ice cream (especially when it was hot). At the station were we stopped, the drinks were placed in a type of soft drink box that they were submerged in ice (mostly cold water). I can remember that the can drinks always had a somewhat musty smell because of that water. I would always try to wipe the top of the can so that you could not smell it, but somehow I always could.

Just as the bus ride to school often accounted for our arriving at school very late, the same was true of the return trip in the evening. Although the usual time for getting home was about 5:00 – 5:30 p.m., it was not unusual to get home after dark during the winter months. This also meant that if there was a mechanical problem, we might have been left on a cold, dark bus. At any rate, this was just part of the price that was paid for wanting to get an education. Although it might have seemed very hard, at the time, it was just part of getting an education.

The Quality of an Education from St. Paul

I guess when measuring the quality of the education gained at St. Paul High School, one has to measure that education with a special gauge. As far as textbook learning, I guess I would say that it was minimal. One reason is that textbooks were outdated and often very worn or in short supply. Equipment, such as typewriters, was so worn out, that it was hard to find one that worked properly in typing class. This was probably due to the fact that they had been discarded from the white schools. (The typing class was taught in the library, which contained old, torn books.) Sometimes there were not enough books, nor other equipment, so the overall environment was not the most conducive for learning. However, with the life's lessons gained at St. Paul and the foundation that I received at Sand Flat, I was indeed prepared for not just college—I was prepared for life!

Chapter 3
About The McMillans

The surname, "McMillan," is of Scotch-Irish descent. There are several variations in the spelling. In fact, my grandfather spelled it McMillian; and several branches of the family spell the name that way today. However, in searching early U.S. Census Records, I found the spellings McMillion, McMillain, McMillian and McMillan for members of my family. Often the same person's name would be spelled differently with each Census. The spelling for my (immediate) family, however, is "McMillan."

Photo of Dora Russell McMillan

My great-grandfather's name was Alfred McMillan. My father was named after him and so was my oldest brother, Alfred. My father chose to use the initials, A.C. Several other McMillans were named Alfred and Acie. I am not sure if that is a derivative or not. My father's brother, P. W. (Preston Winford) also has a name that has been used through the years. He has a daughter, grandson, and nephew with variations of Preston and Winford. My father's brother, S.J., (for Sol Jackson) was named for his grandfather (my paternal grandmother's father). My father's sister, Deora (similar to my great-grandmother, Dora, pictured to the right), has a great granddaughter named after her. And my grandfather, Jewel, has two grandsons named after him—my brother, Jewel, and my cousin Hobert. I, Gwendolyn, was not named after a family member, but there are two Gwendolyns in the family at present. My step-grandmother, Lutishie, had a daughter named Gwendolyn Sue; and my daughter's name is Sylvia Gwen. (By the way, I was not given a middle name.) Perhaps, in some ways, I was lucky not to have a middle name. My grandfather had several brothers and sisters. Unfortunately, my memories of some of them are somewhat vague. For example, my memories of Uncle Nelon are that he was a big teaser. In fact, I can remember being somewhat frightened of him. Uncle Jake (Anon) was often referred to as a teller of tall tales (a polite way of saying that he was a big liar). I had a chance to get to know Uncle Jake better when I attended Henderson County Junior College in Athens, which was where Uncle Jake and his wife Aunt Susie lived. They were always glad to have me visit and went out of their way to make my stay special. Aunt Susie always prepared lots of food for me, and Uncle Jake always gave me extra lunch money. I often spent time with them, especially when I wanted to attend activities at school on the weekends or at night. I can remember that Uncle Hervey had a red house in Greenville. Uncle Hervey was actually my dad's great-uncle. This uncle, I remember most by his house—the red house. Another great-uncle in Mineral Wells, Uncle Arthur, had a hotel. I can't remember much about him, except I remember when he died. I can remember that we made the trip to Mineral Wells for the funeral. I can remember that Aunt Ora (my grandfather's sister) often sat in a chair and slept. I heard people say that she had the "dropsy." Aunt Olma (also my grandfather's sister), who lived to be over 100 years old, is the one that I remember best. When I was growing up in Emory, she attended the McMillan Reunion each year. She lived in Borger, Texas, and she generally stayed a week or so with our family after the Reunion. She often packed boxes of clothing and sent them to us. She would tell my mother, "Modis, if you cannot use them, give them to someone that can. I just hate to see good things go to waste." Another thing that I vividly remember about her is that when she talked to you, she would affectionately tap you on the leg or shoulder to be sure that you were listening. She wrote letters that made you imagine that you were actually listening to her as you read them. She would write one letter over a period of several days. That way she would have more to tell you. And she often wrote my mother letters until she was in her eighties or nineties. Those letters were really essays on the things that were going on in her lifetime.

Olma McMillan Malone

Because during the early years of my life motels, restaurants, etc., were all segregated, most families did not take long trips by automobile. My family, however, took many trips to Borger, Amarillo, Wichita Falls, and Electra, to visit Aunt Olma, her Son (Otto called "Cousin Pat"), and her daughters, Zona (Bit) Coffer and Ruth ("Aunt Sister" Edwards). We packed food and drinks for the road. My mother packed cold cut sandwiches, fried chicken, and sometimes pound cake. These were exciting times in my childhood. We never really focused on what we could not do; we were excited about what we did.

There was an Uncle Johnnie (John Doris), who lived in Kansas City. This was also my grandfather's brother. I don't remember him well. However, I do remember that my father used to go to Kansas City to visit him. I can remember that he went once during the winter and had to drive through the snow to get back home. There is also a story of his wife's wanting to have him cremated; and, of course, in those days that was unheard of in our family. While he was near death, my grandfather, along with some other relatives (my father included), went to Kansas City to visit him. He died while they were there, and he was buried—not cremated.

Of all of the McMillan ancestors, few were really famous. However, I do recall hearing of a Dr. Walter McMillan in Dallas when I was growing up. Also, there was a Dr. Julius McMillan, a black surgeon at Meharry University in Tennessee that I heard about. In recent years, perhaps the most noted family member is Danny Everett, an Olympic Gold Medalist (in track). He is the grandson of Uncle Nelon, the brother of my grandfather. His mother, Willie Grace, was called "Cute Thing" (actually, it was "Cute Thang") when we were growing up.

Early Marriages in the Family

In researching family history, I found that my great grandmother, Dora Russell came from Georgia and married Alfred McMillan in Texas. Alfred's parents were Jake and Mary Jane McMillan. The McMillans settled in Wood County, Texas, before later moving to Rains County. Jake McMillan came from Virginia and Mary Jane came from Tennessee. My grandfather, Jewel McMillan, was born in Texas and was married three times. Although the first wife, Callie Jackson McMillan, was my father's mother, I grew up knowing the second wife, Elberta (Nanaw) as my grandmother. His third wife, Lutishie Smith McMillan, I grew up knowing as "Cousin Lutishie." My father, A. C. McMillan, married my mother in Emory, Texas. Both were from Emory. I grew up in the "Wolf" community; and I now live in Dallas, Texas on "Wolfwood" Lane. My husband, Theodore M. Lawe, and I met in Dallas; married in Emory; and now live in Dallas, Texas. My husband (Ted) is from Tampa, Florida.

Holidays in Our Family

National Holidays such as the Fourth of July, Veterans Day,

Memorial Day, etc., are not celebrated in a big way. The same is true for family birthdays. However, religious holidays—Easter, Christmas, and Thanksgiving—are big family days. Our families have also traditionally celebrated Mother's Day and Father's Day. We have a "holiday dinner" that is served on Christmas, Thanksgiving, Mother's Day, and Easter. This dinner usually consists of turkey and (cornbread) dressing, ham, fresh (or frozen) peas, candied yams, and a holiday "pink salad." I first made this salad as a part of the holiday meal, but it has been passed on to my daughter now and it is her contribution to making the holiday meal. There are many recipes that have been passed on from my mother to me. This one is the one that I have passed on to my daughter. The recipe for the Pink Salad is below:

Recipe for "Pink Salad"
Combine the following ingredients:
1 can cherry pie filling (strawberry pie filling may be substituted)
1 container of Cool Whip
1 can Eagle Brand (condensed, sweetened) milk
1 can crushed pineapple
1 cup coconut
1 cup pecans
1 can fruit cocktail

- Other items can be added according to taste—miniature marshmallows, Mandarin oranges, bananas, etc. Also, to achieve a fluffier salad, additional Cool Whip can be added.

With this meal, there are usually such things as rolls, iced tea, and several desserts. But the desserts are usually eaten later, because we are all usually too stuffed for dessert after such a meal.

Jewel McMillan

The Third Sunday (now the Third Saturday) is a family holiday. For over 50 years, the McMillan Family Reunion has been held on this date. The Reunion has always been held in Emory, Texas. My grandfather, Jewel McMillan, started the Reunion. He said that he wanted to do something for the family to get together other than at funerals. Today the Reunion is carried on by the Jewel McMillan children (daughters- and sons-in-law) and grandchildren. Each year the Reunion is dedicated to someone who has had a positive impact on the event. In 2005, the Reunion held its 50th Anniversary Celebration and honored all of the daughters, daughters-in-law, and sons-in-law as Torchbearers for carrying on the tradition of the McMillan Family Reunion for 50 years.

Chapter 4
The Genealogy Of The McMillan Family Of Emory, Texas

Alfred (A.C.) McMillan was born April 23, 1855, the son of Jake McMillan and Mary Jane McMillan. On May 3, 1876, Alfred McMillan of Texas and Dora Russell (born May 11, 1856) of Georgia were married by Elder W. Peterson at the home of Henry Peterson. The witnesses were Sarah Baily and W. Flourney. A. C. and Dora McMillan came to Emory from Quitman, Texas with Dick ("Little Dick," is what I am told that my grandfather referred to him as) McMillan. A. C. and Dora McMillan were the first black schoolteachers in Emory. However, according to Commissioner's Court Minutes dated June 1895, A. C. McMillan was appointed a trustee of school district #1 (col.), which I presume meant "colored."

THE CHILDREN OF ALFRED AND DORA *McMillan*
- Perla Cordela McMillan was born May 21, 1877.
- Arthur Soney Wilson McMillan was born October 13, 1879.

49

- John Doris McMillan was born November 28, 1881.
- Dalia Harriett McMillan was born April 12, 1884. (Aunt Olma always said that I, Gwendolyn, was just like her sister, Dalia.)
- James Burnice McMillan was born March 16, 1886.
- Olma Isola McMillan was born March 20, 1891.
- Alfred Eddie McMillan was born September 20, 1893.
- **Jewel Hobert McMillan (my grandfather) was born April 16, 1896.**
- Anon McMillan was born September 8, 1900.

These were the brothers and sisters of Jewel McMillan. Alfred (A.C.) married Hattie Williams on April 5, 1914[5]. I am not exactly sure which Alfred (A.C.) this was. If this was my great-grandfather, he would have been 60 at the time. However, if this was referring to Alfred Eddie McMillan, he would have been 21.

ANON "JAKE" MCMILLAN

Anon "Jake" McMillan was born September 8, 1900, to Alfred and Dora McMillan. He was married to Susie McMillan, who preceded him in death. At the time of his death, December 16, 1981, one sister, Olma Malone, survived him. However, she died in 1988 (over a hundred years old). He had been a long-time resident of Athens, Texas. When I attended Henderson County Junior College (now Trinity Valley Community College), I really got to know "Uncle Jake" and "Aunt Susie" very well. They always encouraged me to stay in school and to get an education. However, they were not fond of my socializing with other young people from Athens. "Uncle Jake" always said that if I, or any of his relatives, would get a degree in medicine, he would pay for us to go to college. I majored in business education,

---

5 Taken from the Bible of my grandfather's sister, Olma Malone.

so I did not get to take him up on his offer. However, he and his wife were very helpful to me and I often stayed with them in Athens. I can remember once that he had me close his checking account in Emory. He told me that I could have the balance—I did not know that it was only a few dollars. But just the same, it was all mine.

ANON MCMILLAN AND SUSIE MCMILLAN HAD NO CHILDREN.

ARTHUR WILSON MCMILLAN

Arthur Wilson McMillan was born to Alfred and Dora McMillan on October 13, 1879, in Quitman, Texas. He later moved to Mineral Wells. He married Lena English, of Greenville, Texas, who died in 1992. They had one daughter. Arthur McMillan died on March 5, 1963. At the time of his death, one sister, Olma Malone, survived him along with two brothers: Jewel McMillan and Anon McMillan; and one son and one daughter.

THE CHILDREN OF ARTHUR WILSON MCMILLAN

- Velma Reed.
- Herman McMillan.

DALIA MCMILLAN JACKSON (MARRIED TO WALTER JACKSON)

Dalia McMillan Jackson was born April 12, 1884, to Alfred and Dora McMillan. Dalia (the sister that "Aunt Olma" and "Daddy Jewel" said that I was like) was married to Walter Jackson.

THE CHILDREN OF DALIA MCMILLAN JACKSON

- Roosevelt Ted Jackson, born November 11, 1906; died April 10, 1977. Ted is the father of Roosevelt "Gummy" Jackson, a strong supporter of the McMillan Reunion.

- Zelma Murray, deceased.
- Pollie Andrews, deceased.
- Lois Fay McGruder (the grandmother of Christy McGruder), resided in Fort Worth, Texas; deceased.
- Leon Jackson.
- Claud Jackson.
- Elma Jackson.

PERLA CORDELA MCMILLAN

Perla Cordela McMillan was born May 21, 1877, to Alfred and Dora McMillan. Perla McMillan married Sam Dean. Perla McMillan Dean raised Obie Dean (Robinson), her grandson, (son of Lonnie Robinson).

CHILDREN OF PERLA CORDELA MCMILLAN DEAN

- * Clide Dean, died August 28, 1900.
- * Hobbie Dean, deceased. (Wife's name is Gladys.)
- * Dock Dean, deceased. (Wife's name: JoJo.)
- * Oney Dean had no children.
- * Lynn Dean had no children.
- * Ethel Dean.
- * Dora Dean Eggleston had no children.
- * Josephine Dean Robinson Gibson.

JOHN DORIS MCMILLAN

John Doris McMillan was born November 28, 1881, to Alfred and Dora McMillan. John McMillan was married to Montegg McMillan. Uncle "Johnny" lived in Kansas City, Missouri at the time of his death. However, he was buried in Emory, Texas.

CHILDREN OF JOHN DORIS MCMILLAN

Alfred Otis McMillan, born May 18, 1907; died December 5, 1907. He had two daughters Mable McMillan and Tamara McMillan.

JAMES BERNICE MCMILLAN

James Bernice McMillan was born March 15, 1886 to Alfred and Dora McMillan. James Bernice McMillan married Theodora Smith. They had two children: Lottie Ruth and James Bernice. Another son, Lawrence McMillan (died in 1987) was raised by the Deans until he was about 5. James Bernice and family lived in Mineral Wells, Texas. He died in October of 1941. Lottie Ruth now lives in Denver, Colorado and James Bernice (son of James Bernice) lives in Richmond, California. Thanks to Lottie (via telephone conversations), I was able to attain some family history that I did not have.

ALFRED EDDIE MCMILLAN

Alfred Eddie McMillan was born September 20, 1893, to Alfred and Dora McMillan. This is all that is known about Alfred Eddie McMillan, except that he was married and had no children.

OLMA ISOLA MCMILLAN MALONE
(MARRIED TO CHARLIE "BUD" MALONE)

Olma McMillan Malone was born in Emory, Texas, September 7, 1888, to Alfred and Dora McMillan. She married Charlie "Bud" Malone in Emory, Texas. To this marriage two sons and three daughters were born. One son, James, preceded her in death. Olma McMillan Malone died February 15, 1990, in Borger, Texas, where she had lived for a number of years. At the time of her death, she was survived by one son, Otto "Pat" Malone of Electra, Texas (who is now deceased); three daughters: Minnie Fields of Lakeview Terrace, California; Zona Coffer and Ruth Edward of Borger, Texas; fourteen grandchildren; twenty-one great grandchildren; seventeen great-great grandchildren; and two great-great-great grandchildren. "Aunt Olma" was a supporter of the Reunion and attended each year until shortly before her death, when her health would no longer allow her to attend. Her children, the Malones, now have an annual reunion also.

THE CHILDREN OF OLMA ISOLA MCMILLAN MALONE (MARRIED TO CHARLIE MALONE)

- Otto "Pat" Malone, deceased.
- Minnie Malone Fields, deceased
- Ruth "Sister" Malone Edwards, deceased.
- James "Brother" Malone, deceased.
- Zona "Bit" Coffer.

ORA VISTA MCMILLAN MURRAY (MARRIED TO FRAZIER MURRAY)

Ora Vista McMillan Murray was born March 20, 1891, the daughter of Alfred and Dora McMillan. She married Frazier Murray. Ora and Frazier had eight children. Both lived in Emory at the time of their deaths. One son, Vernon, remained in Emory.

THE CHILDREN OF ORA VISTA MCMILLAN MURRAY

- Alene Murray
- Vernon Murray, deceased.
- Rachel "Dollie" Murray Robinson, deceased.
- Vaudie Murray Calhoun.
- Eldora "Sissy" Murray Bobo.

- Dorothy Murray Tolliver, deceased.
- Henry Murray, deceased.
- Harvey Murray, deceased.

JEWEL HOBERT MCMILLAN
(THE PATRIACH OF THE MCMILLANS OF EMORY)

Jewel Hobert McMillan, born to Alfred (A.C.) and Dora McMillan, was born April 18, 1896, in Emory, Rains County, Texas. He united with the Hopewell Baptist Church then later with the Prairie Grove Baptist Church. He was married to Callie Jackson and Elberta Woosley. Both preceded him in death. At the time of his death, October 11, 1976, he was married to Lutishie McMillan, who died in March of 1998. At the time of his death, he was survived by four sons, five daughters, six stepsons, six stepdaughters, 35 grandchildren, and 60 great-grandchildren, and one great-great-grandchild. A lifetime citizen of Rains County, most people in the community affectionately referred to him as "Daddy Jewel," which is what all of his grandchildren called him. "Daddy Jewel" began the McMillan Reunion in or about 1954. This McMillan Reunion has been held continuously since that time. Each year the Reunion is dedicated to someone that has been instrumental in making the McMillan Reunion a success. Some of those that the Reunion was first dedicated to were: Otto Malone, son of Olma Malone, and "Boots" and Florene McMillan. Some of the most recent were: Joe Jones, Jr., (who passed in May of 1998) son of Modean Lane; Gwendolyn McMillan Lawe, daughter of A.C. and Modis McMillan; Debra McMillan Twitty, daughter of P.W. and Claressa McMillan; Emma McMillan Madlock, daughter of "Boots" and Florene McMillan; Delenis Garrett, son of Dave and Mildred Garrett; and Fannie Garrett Brown, daughter of Fannon and Deora

Garrett. The 2004 McMillan Reunion was dedicated to Willie Grace McMillan. These are just to name a few. The Reunion was held in Emory, Texas, on the third Sunday in July for many years. In 1998 it was changed to the Saturday before the third Sunday. The McMillan Family carries out this tradition that Jewel McMillan started.

THE CHILDREN OF JEWEL MCMILLAN

- Irene Thornton Robinson, deceased.
- Elbert (Boots) McMillan, deceased.
- Alfred Clifton (A.C.) McMillan, deceased.
- Modean Abernathy Lane.
- Loretta Porter Williams, deceased.
- Mildred McMillan Garrett.
- Deora McMillan Garrett, deceased
- P. W. McMillan, deceased.
- S. J. McMillan, deceased.
- John Wesley Thomas (son of Elberta), deceased.

DESCENDANT OF JEWEL MCMILLAN
ALFRED CLIFTON (A.C.) MCMILLAN

Alfred Clifton (A.C.) McMillan was born December 28, 1921, to Jewel McMillan and Callie Jackson McMillan. A. C. McMillan married Modis Robinson of Emory, Texas on November 16, 1942.

A.C. graduated from Texas College in Tyler, Texas, after serving in the United States Army. A.C. was the first (and only) of Jewel and Callie's children to obtain a college education. He did graduate work at Prairie View A & M College, Texas Southern University, and received a Master's Degree from East Texas State University. He was a principal and teacher at Sand Flat School until its closing in 1969 and retired from Rains Junior High School in 1985 after 36 years service to the education of Rains County youths.

While at Sand Flat School, he provided students with more than an education from books. Students from Sand Flat traveled to Prairie View to attend state UIL meetings back when we referred to it as attending "The League." Several of the children of the Hunter family and Edwin Collins were among those who attended those contests. Sand Flat students took a train ride (from Mineola to Dallas), visited radio stations, and participated in other educational activities, as a result of the efforts of A.C. McMillan. An anonymous donor once funded a tour to Mexico for the students of Sand Flat; and, yes, it was A.C. McMillan who drove the bus and gave many young children (and adults) an opportunity to visit outside the United States for the first time and their first opportunity to stay in motels and eat in restaurants.

He was also known for his community service. He was Sunday School Superintendent and a trustee at the Prairie Grove Baptist Church for many years. He served on many civic boards such as the Mental Health and Mental Retardation (MHMR) and NET Opportunities. He was instrumental in helping many youth and adults gain employment both on a part-time and a permanent basis. And countless numbers of students were able to attend college because of his guidance and assistance. He helped them fill out the applications and often carried them to the campus.

A.C. was also a car salesman in his spare time—having worked for several dealerships over the years. In fact, he probably sold more cars (new and used) than any other person in Rains County during the sixties, seventies, and early eighties.

A.C. McMillan died on November 7, 1985, in the Veteran's Administration Hospital in Dallas, Texas. In 1987, the McMillan Family started **The A. C. McMillan Scholarship**, which is awarded annually to students at Rains High School. To date, many Rains students have been the recipients of this award.

These are the children of A.C. McMillan and Modis McMillan: Alfred Clifton McMillan, born June 3, 1945; Gwendolyn McMillan Lawe, born February 3, 1948; Jewel Henry McMillan, born November 24, 1949; and Harold Dale McMillan, born January 31, 1957.

Alfred McMillan married Altha Taylor of Longview, Texas. Alfred resides in Emory. He has two daughters: Yolanda Edwards and April Carol McMillan. He has four grandchildren and three great-grandchildren.

I, Gwendolyn McMillan married Theodore M. Lawe of Tampa. We have two children: Theodore M. Lawe, III (Tony) and Sylvia Lawe. We have six grandchildren. Tony lives in Newark, New Jersey and Sylvia and her husband, Jerry Williams, and sons Preston and Blair live in Longview, Texas.

Jewel Henry McMillan lives in Lake Jackson, Texas. Jewel has one daughter, Stacye McMillan Hargrove, and three grandchildren who live in Houston, Texas.

Harold Dale McMillan lives in Austin, Texas. Harold has one son, Hayes Michael McMillan.

DESCENDANTS OF JEWEL MCMILLAN
ELBERT "BOOTS" MCMILLAN

Elbert "Boots" McMillan was born March 26, 1920, to Jewel McMillan and Callie Jackson McMillan in Emory, Texas. He attended Sand Flat Public School and was a member of the Prairie Grove Baptist Church, serving as President of the Senior Usher Board, member of the Trustee Board, and a member of the Prairie Grove Masonic Lodge #185. He was also a member of Rio-Grand Lodge Chapter 105, where he held the office of High Priest.

Elbert McMillan married Florene Blaylock on December 25, 1940. Elbert "Boots" McMillan died September 22, 1985.

Emma Jean McMillan Madlock of Tyler, Texas was the oldest daughter of Elbert and Florene McMillan. Emma married Darryl Madlock. Their children are, Felecia, who is married to Brian Keith Thomas; Jennifer, who is married to Tyronne Petiford; and Darryl Madlock is married to Twania. Emma had twelve grandchildren.

Emma Madlock died in December of 1995 in Tyler, Texas, after a lengthy illness.

Juanita McMillan Briggs lived in Missouri City, Texas at the time of her death. She was married to Donald Briggs. They have one daughter, Krystal Briggs.

Troy Elbert McMillan was the older son of Elbert and Florene McMillan. Troy was married to Swaunice Bozman McMillan and they lived in Emory, Texas at the time of his death. They have three children: Shajuana, Derrick, who is married to Leslie; and Angela, who is married to Tyronne Ventors. Troy and Swaunice have eight grandchildren.

Kenneth McMillan the younger son of Elbert and Florene McMillan, is also deceased. He was married to Edna Johnson McMillan at the time of his death. They have a number of children; Bridgette, who is married to Josquin Underwood, Stacye, who is married to Aaron Hargrove; Joshua, who is married to Konnett, Joel and Lyndsey. Kenneth and Edna had six grandchildren when I gathered this information. They resided in Richmond, Texas at the time of his death.

Dianne McMillan Crowe is the youngest and only living of the children of Elbert and Florene McMillan. She is married to Archie Crowe of Knoxville, Tennessee. They reside in Arlington, Texas.

DESCENDANTS OF JEWEL MCMILLAN
P. W. MCMILLAN

SUNRISE: July 25, 1929

SUNSET: June 17, 2002

P.W. McMillan was born to Jewel McMillan and Callie Jackson McMillan on July 25, 1929. P. W. McMillan married Claressa Cooks of Calvert, Texas, on December 25, 1953. They both resided in Emory, Texas at the time of his death in 2002. For years, P.W. was a truckdriver and drove throughout the United States. It was because of him that several of his nephews also chose to become truckdrivers. Claressa was a licensed beautician and practiced this trade for many years. She was one of the few licensed hairdressers in the African American community in Emory for many years. Claressa lived in Emory until she died in July of 2010. One son died at birth, Larry Preston McMillan.

DESCENDANTS OF P.W. MCMILLAN
Debra Jo McMillan Twitty is the oldest child of P.W. and

Claressa McMillan. Debra is married to Kenneth Twitty. They have three daughters: Morgan, Meghan, and McKenzie. They live in Missouri City, Texas. The 1996 McMillan Reunion was dedicated to Debra Jo Twitty.

Winford Jean McMillan Goodman, the younger daughter of P.W. and Claressa McMillan, was married to Harold Goodman of Beaumont, Texas. Jean and Harold have two sons: Harold Preston and Winston Eugene Goodman. Jean lives in Houston, Texas. "Jean" (as we all call her) and family have moved around a lot because of her and her husband's being employed by Federal Express. I have visited with her at three different homes in the Houston, Texas area and in Florida.

Clifford Eugene McMillan, born February 18, 1969, is the youngest child of P.W. and Claressa McMillan. Clifford married Angela Taylor McMillan. Clifford has two children: Shatoya McMillan and Clifford Eugene McMillan. Clifford now resides in Cypress, Texas.

DESCENDANTS OF JEWEL MCMILLAN

Deora McMillan Garrett (far right)

DEORA (MCMILLAN) GARRETT

Deora McMillan Garrett was born to Jewel McMillan and Calllie Jackson McMillan on March 2, 1926, in Emory, Texas. Deora McMillan married Fannon Garrett on May 30, 1946. Deora was a member of Prairie Grove Baptist Church and also a member of the Center Point Court #123, of the Heroines of Jericho. Deora McMillan Garrett died on September 15, 1993. One son, Leslie Floyd Garrett, preceded her in death.

DESCENDANTS OF DEORA (MCMILLAN) GARRETT

Marcus D. Garrett, the oldest child of Deora and Fannon Garrett, is married to Doris Garrett. Marcus is a graduate of Rains High School and attended Henderson County Junior College. Marcus and Doris have three sons, Clinton, Clavin, and Xavier, and four grandchildren.

J.W. Garrett, the second son of Deora and Fannon Garrett, is married to Laverne Garrett. They live in Cedar Hill. They have two children, DeAndra Garrett (who lives in Irving) and Christopher. Christopher and his wife (April) have two sons, Quentin and Christian. They live in Saganaw.

Fannie M. Garrett Brown, daughter of Deora and Fannon Garrett is married to Ronnie Brown, of Birmingham, Alabama. Fannie and Ronnie Brown live in Rowlett, Texas. They have three children, LaFeyshia Meador (who attended Talladega College); KaVayshia Meador-Allison (who attended Grambling State University); and Fannon LaRay Meador, who served in the United States Marine Corps. Fannie has eight grandchildren.

Leslie Floyd Garrett (deceased) married Delores Boyce of Emory. They had six children: Shaquila Garrett, Rodrian Garrett, Marquisha Garrett, Leslie LaTrevis Garrett, Lauston Garrett, and Leslie Floyd Garrett, Jr., all of Emory, and several grandchildren.

Irene Thornton Robinson

(Front row: Center)

IRENE THORNTON ROBINSON

Irene Thornton Robinson was born to Callie Jackson and Herman Thornton on July 18, 1915. She attended the Sand Flat School and was a member of Prairie Grove Baptist Church in Emory, Texas. Irene ("Cooksie") Thornton married Hubert (Stew) Robinson of Emory. Irene and Hubert were parents of seven children. One child preceded her in death. Irene Thornton Robinson died on October 18, 1977. Hubert Robinson died on August 14, 1989.

DESCENDANTS OF IRENE THORNTON (MCMILLAN) ROBINSON

Callie Robinson Johnson, the oldest daughter of Hubert and Irene Robinson is deceased. She had one son, Edwin. Edwin married

Patricia Kelly Robinson of Emory. They have one daughter. Edwin lives in Point, Texas.

Herman Robinson is the oldest son of Hubert and Irene Robinson. He resides in Emory.

John L. Robinson is married to Rose McGill Robinson. They have four children and several grandchildren. They live in Como, Texas.

Hubert Robinson, Jr., is married to Willie Bozman Robinson. They have four children and several grandchildren. They live in Emory.

Ellen (Gladys) McKnight, daughter of Hubert and Irene Robinson, lives in Garland, Texas.

Vannie M. Robinson Miles, the youngest of the Irene Robinson children, married Willie D. Miles. They have two daughters. Vannie lives in Emory.

Modean Abernathy Lane McMillan

(Front row: left)

DESCENDANTS OF JEWEL MCMILLAN
MODEAN ABERNATHY (MCMILLAN) LANE

Modean Abernathy was born to Jewel McMillan and Euna Abernathy on February 4, 1920. Modean married Joe Jones. She later married Willie Lane. Joe Jones and Willie Lane are deceased. Modean attended Sand Flat School and is an active member of the Prairie Grove Baptist Church. She has worked in many auxiliaries of the church.

DESCENDANTS OF MODEAN (MCMILLAN) LANE

Joe Jones, Jr., the oldest child of Modean Lane, passed in May of 1998. The fortieth McMillan Family Reunion (1995) was dedicated to Joe Jones, Jr. for his dedicated service and work with the McMillan Reunion. Joe was a graduate of Texas College, Tyler, Texas; and he held a Master's Degree from Texas Southern University, in Houston, Texas. Joe married Dorothy Jones. For years, Joe and Dorothy hosted a New Year's Eve party at their home. I looked forward to this annual event. He and Dorothy have two children, Jill and Tony. They have two grandchildren. Joe lived in Duncanville, Texas at the time of his death.

Telesta Jones Riggs is the older daughter of Modean Lane. She is married to Earl Riggs. They have three daughters and two grandchildren. They live in Springfield, Virginia.

Alton Ray Jones, son of Modean Lane, married Dorothy Miles Jones of Emory. They have four children and three grandchildren. They lived in Houston, Texas at the time of her death in 2009.

Tredis Jones Griffin, younger daughter of Modean Lane, married to Ben Griffin. She is retired from the Dallas Public Schools. Ben died in 2010. They have two daughters and a grandson. They live in DeSoto, Texas.

Norris W. Lane, son of Modean Lane, married Gwendolyn Smith Lane. They have two children and two grandchildren. Norris lives in Emory.

Jerry Lane, son of Modean Lane, married Wilma Boyce Lane. They have six children and several grandchildren. They lived n Emory at the time of his death in 2006.

DESCENDANTS OF JEWEL MCMILLAN

Mildred McMillan Garrett (Front row, third from left)

MILDRED (MCMILLAN) GARRETT

Mildred McMillan Garrett was born to Jewel McMillan and Callie Jackson McMillan on September 5, 1923. Mildred attended Sand Flat School and is a member of Prairie Grove Baptist Church. Mildred served in the military and since that time has resided in Emory. She is very active in the church and in the community. She served for several years on the Emory City Council (also served as

Mayor Pro Tem), a position that had not been held by an African American female (and has not been held by another). She worked for many years for the United States Postal Service. She retired from the Postal Service in 1998. Mildred McMillan married David Garrett, who died in 2010. They have five sons and several grandchildren and great-grandchildren.

DESCENDANTS OF MILDRED (MCMILLAN) GARRETT

James Hobert Bates is the oldest son of Mildred McMillan Garrett. James retired from the United States Army and resided in Valejo, California for many years. He married Mamie Bates. They have two sons and five grandchildren. James Hobert Bates now lives in Oregon.

David Gearld Garrett, son of Mildred and David Garrett, is also retired from the United States Army. David is married to Clemmie Gilstrap Garrett of Greenville, Texas. They have two children and two grandchildren. They reside in Bedford, Texas.

Howard Preston Garrett, son of Mildred and David Garrett, married Glenda Givens Garrett from Point, Texas. They have three daughters and six grandchildren. They live in Arlington, Texas.

Delenis Garrett, son of Mildred and David Garrett, married Ava Garrett. They have one son, Nicholas. Delenis lives in Tyler, Texas. Delenis is married to Nikita Johnson Garrett. They have one son Antoine and a grandaughter, Nicole.

Thomas (Tony) Edwin Garrett, youngest of the Garrett sons, is married to Dendra Dial Garrett of Sulphur Springs, Texas. "Tony" has four children and three grandchildren. Tony and his family live in Mesquite, Texas.

Mildred and David Garrett also raised a grandson, Undray Smallwood, and later adopted him. He is the son of Tony Garrett.

Chapter 5
The Jacksons Of Emory, Texas

It would be hard to write my family's history without including the Jacksons and how I am related to the Jacksons. My father's mother, Callie Jackson McMillan, was the first wife of my grandfather, Jewel McMillan. Her father, Sol Jackson (my great-grandfather), was said to have come to Emory with Emory Rains for whom Emory and Rains are named. Sol Jackson was married to Hanna Jackson. The siblings of my grandmother were: Emory ("Em") Jackson (who was married to Georgia Jackson and father of George Jackson, Helen Jackson, and Josie Mae Hampton), Nellie Jackson Snell (mother of Lorine Sims, Viola Brackeen who married K.B. Brackeen, and Johnny Snell who married Lucille Snell), Haywood Jackson (married Gracie Jackson), Johnny Jackson, Ben Jackson, Tinnie Jackson, and Velma Jackson Davis (married Manuel Davis).

Although I do not remember my grandmother, I do remember some of her siblings. For example, when I was growing up in Emory, our family often visited Uncle Emory ("Em") and his wife, Georgia, in Dallas. I can remember spending time with them during summer vacation. They also owned a home in Emory. Their children were

71

named George (Jr.), Josie Mae, and Helen. George still lives in Dallas. I think that Helen lives in Colorado. Josie Mae is deceased. Aunt Nellie lived in Jacksonville when I was growing up and I also can remember spending time at her house—on Sundays after church and overnights. The Jackson Reunion is held at her home place today. Her daughter, Viola Brackeen, was the individual who conceived the idea of having a Jackson Family Reunion. She also had another daughter, Lorene Simms, who resided in a Sulphur Springs nursing home for several years prior to her death in 2009. Uncle Haywood was married to Aunt Gracie Jackson. I hardly remember Uncle Haywood, but Aunt Gracie lived until 1999. She was the matriarch of the Jackson Family. In fact, her birthday was celebrated by the family somewhat as a holiday. It was a family reunion. Aunt Gracie and Uncle Haywood had a very large family and I cannot name all of them; however, because several lived in the community and the surrounding towns, I can remember them best. For example, Betty Jackson Heard lived in Jacksonville until her recent death in 1999 when she was killed in an automobile accident. One son, Wallace, was in school with my brother Alfred; and one sister, Helen, was in school with me. Wallace Jackson married Ruthie "Sis" Hunter. They live in San Antonio, Texas. Helen lives in Greenville. A brother, Leroy Jackson and his wife Martha moved to San Antonio, Texas when I was very young. Otha Lee ("Peal") Jackson and his wife Betty (Boyd) Jackson were our next-door neighbors when their children were very small. I was very young at this time also. Betty passed in 2004. Another sister, Nellie, lived in Greenville (and still does). I can remember that she lived near my mother's sister, Aunt Virgie. Another brother, Jessie Lee Jackson, lived in Lone Oak. He and his wife moved to Emory several years ago and were living in Emory at the time of his death in 2004. When I was in elementary and high school, his daughters took music lessons from the same music teacher that I did. I didn't really know them, but I would see them at Mrs. Lewis's on Saturdays. And there was another sister, Annie Ruth Jackson Pickrom, who has now moved back to Emory and resides in the Jacksonville Community. I used to see her at reunions, but I did not know her very well. Hannah Bell Jackson McMillan was married to my father's uncle, Nelon McMillan. They lived in Emory for a number of years. However, after the death of Uncle Nelon, the family moved to Fresno, California. Hannah lived in California until her death. Lutishie Jackson Smith McMillan was also a daughter of Haywood and Gracie Jackson. She was married to R. P. Smith. She later married my grandfather, Jewel McMillan.

Chapter 6
The Robinsons Of Emory, Texas

My mother, Modis Robinson McMillan, was born in Emory, Texas. Unfortunately, I do not have a lot of information on the Robinsons beyond my great-grandparents. My great-grandparents were Samson "Pete" and Martha Gee Bridges. Pete Bridges was from Springfield,

Missouri. Pete Bridges came to town with the Woosley Family. Although I have rarely heard it mentioned, he was blind. Like most slaves, the name Bridges came from his slave master. He married Hattie Turner after the death of wife, Martha. Hattie died in 1937.

The children of Pete and Martha Bridges were: Lena, Tennie, Alice, and Lucy (my grandmother, pictured above). I do not remember any of my grandmother's siblings, however, I do remember talk of Aunt Alice's moving away and never being heard from until long after her death. I can remember when I was in college a "Cousin Claudia" coming to visit from Detroit. She was the daughter of my Aunt Alice, whom my mother's family had not heard from since she left Texas. Cousin Claudia had invited me to visit her in Detroit. I was really looking forward to that visit. Cousin Claudia died shortly after I met her. My grandparents were Henry and Lucy Robinson. As far as I know, they were both from Emory. My grandfather, Henry, died before I was born (in 1944). His parents were John and Sara Robinson.

Although these were his "parents," supposedly, his biological father was named Spradling, a white man. At present, I have not been able to confirm his first name. This was very common during this time. Even though I never knew my grandfather, I do remember my grandmother, Lucy, very well. She died when I was in the tenth grade (1963).

Some of my memories of my grandmother ("Mama Lucy") include our families having dinner at her house on special days. I can remember that as a small child I had to stand during dinner. I also remember the large tumblers (drinking glasses) that the adults used while the children drank their tea or Kool-Aid from "snuff" glasses. Yes, during this time, many older people dipped snuff and it came in small cans or larger glasses. It was always very special when I visited Mama Lucy and got to drink from the large tumblers. In fact, when I became an adult and got my own apartment, I bought a couple of those tumblers. These kinds of tumblers are used today in bars as "beer mugs" but I still remember how good the iced tea and Kool-Aid tasted when drank from those glasses at Mama Lucy's house. Mama Lucy also had several things that she would cook especially for me. Another thing that I remember is Mama Lucy's yard. Back then, no one had gardeners, but she had some of the most beautiful flowers. The hickory nut and walnut trees were at Uncle Lonnie and Aunt Matt's house (next door). Looking back, I don't think that I know of any nut (or anything else) that requires as much work to get so little to eat as hickory nuts and black walnuts. The interesting thing is that I only have memories of those nuts because it has been years since I have seen or eaten them. However, recently, Blue Bell ice cream came out with a black walnut flavored ice cream. I was anxious to try it just for the nostalgia—a chance to taste black walnuts again. And, yes, the taste was great, just as I could remember black walnuts.

There are so many things about visiting my grandmother that I still remember that neither time nor paper will allow me to write—the watermelons and cantaloupes in the fields, the fresh tomatoes, and who could forget the sweet potatoes. I think that because I saw so many sweet potato pies then, I do not care very much for them today. However, I "love" candied yams. Also, since this was a time before canned biscuits and instant pancake mix, Mama Lucy would make "hocakes." This was (I think) making homemade biscuits and cooking them in the skillet similar to pancakes. I never learned to make them, but I do remember how good they were and how special it was to request hocakes and have them made just for me! With jelly (homemade), it was a real treat! Mama Lucy made blackberry jelly and jam, plum jelly, and peach and pear preserves. She would also make peach and pear jelly by cooking the peels from the fruit. (This would have usually been discarded.) Of course this tradition of cooking was carried down through the years to her daughters and to this granddaughter. I still make pear preserves and plum jelly.

The children of Henry and Lucy Robinson:
- Elma Robinson Hobbs (deceased)
- Ozell Robinson (deceased)
- Lonnie Robinson (deceased)
- Virgie Robinson Potter (deceased)
- Loda Robinson Kendrick (deceased)
- Lorenza Robinson (deceased)
- Gletha Robinson Davis
- Choycie Robinson (deceased)
- Modis Robinson McMillan (my mother)

Elma Robinson Hobbs, the oldest of the Robinson siblings, married Elbert Hobbs from Richland. He died before I was born or while I was very young. Aunt "Sister," as we called her, was a widow as long as I can remember. Her children are: Famous Hobbs, Anna Hobbs Stokes,

Elvin Hobbs, Lee Hobbs, and Patricia Hobbs Lloyd (deceased). As a child, I was very close to Patricia. (We called her "Sue.") This was because of the closeness of our ages. Sue was killed in a car accident a few years ago. As an adult, I have become closer with Anna, whom we called "Sally." (I am not sure how they got "Sally and Sue" from their names.) Sally only lives a few minutes from me now. We do not visit nor talk on the phone often, but we are still very close.

Because Uncle Lonnie and Aunt Mattie ("Matt") lived next to Mama Lucy, I spent a lot of time at their house while growing up. Their daughter, Doris, spent lots of time with me—doing my hair, etc. I was always very fond of her. I always thought that I was her favorite "little" cousin, since she was much older. When I was 12, I can remember that she baked a cake for my birthday. That was really special! At that time, we really never made much of a fuss over birthdays, but I remember that she baked a cake for me.

Uncle Ozell ("Zell") was married to Annie Woosley Robinson. He was also called "Barber." He did not have a barbershop; he did his work at his house, which was common for that period of time. He did have a barber's chair, but I am not sure if he was licensed or not! He was a very colorful character, using many expletives that only he could use in such a way that he did not seem angry. For years, he cut the hair of most of the African American men and boys in Rains County. He was one of the first African Americans to work for the Texas Highway Department in Emory, also.

The Children of Ozell and Annie Robinson were Delma Robinson (deceased) and Clarelle Robinson. Today, Clarelle lives in Gainesville, Texas.

My Aunt Virgie Robinson Potter was married to Orie Potter. They lived in Greenville, Texas. After his death, however, she moved to Emory. This is where she was living at the time of her death. Since

Aunt Virgie and Uncle Orie lived in Greenville, this was a place that I often spent my vacation time. It was really nice to stay with them. Uncle Orie always called their guest room "Gwen's room," even after I became an adult and had my own home. They had pigeons when I was young. In fact, we once had several pigeons that we had gotten from them. They also ran a store located near their home. In this store, shoppers could buy grocery items. However, I can remember that the children of the neighborhood bought candy, gum, cookies, soft drinks, ice cream, etc. I got lots of pleasure being able to help in the store during my visits. The Potters had no children, so during the illness and death of Uncle Orie, I was very proud to be able to help Aunt Virgie in handling her business affairs. She did not drive, so I enjoyed driving for her. I also can remember that when they were rebricking their home, Uncle Orie, Aunt Virgie, and I came to Dallas to shop for brick. Uncle Orie at the time was in his late 70's. He really astonished the salespeople when he knew the kind of bricks that he wanted. He had drawn a blueprint and he knew exactly how many bricks were needed. I also was amazed at this knowledge. Aunt Virgie had always been a housewife. Uncle Orie was the first African American to work at the U.S. Post Office in Greenville (having made a high score on the test). He often spoke of how he outscored the whites on the test. However, even though he outscored the whites that took the test and was a college graduate, he worked in the mailroom. He was also a minister and Aunt Virgie was the church musician when he was pastor of his church. I don't have a vivid memory of the church services, but I do remember that we always prayed at home at night and he always said long graces before meals.

Loda Robinson Kendrick married Harvey Kendrick. I think that he was from the Como community. Their children are: Harold (Harl) Murray (deceased), Lorretta Kendrick, Delores Kendrick Curtis, Ben

Kendrick, and Deon Kendrick. Aunt Loda lived in Oakland, California, for many years. She and her family later moved to Los Angeles, California. It was always a fun and exciting time when they would visit Mama Lucy. It was at that time that I felt that Los Angeles was the place to be. Aunt Loda's children were very uncomfortable visiting in the country—not having all of the conveniences of the city for which they were accustomed. As an adult, I had a special relationship with Aunt Loda. My cousin, Diane McMillan (Crowe), and I often visited her during the summers. She really enjoyed entertaining us. She would always make a pot of coffee in the evenings when we sat around and talked and she always enjoyed cooking for us. I don't think that any of her children appreciated the coffee in the evenings like we did. She would always laugh and say "for each cup of coffee you put one spoon of coffee and one spoon for the pot, as Grandpa (Pete Bridges) would say." Her granddaughter, Tomia (Loretta's daughter), often visited me in Dallas; and she spent time visiting my parents in Emory. In fact, she even went to school at Rains for a while. At one time, I considered allowing Tomia to live with me permanently. That was when I was single and was not a mother at the time. Aunt Loda's dream was to move back to Emory. She bought a house, had it remodeled, but unfortunately she died before she had a chance to realize that dream. Her children did, however, bring her body back to be buried in Emory. Even though they were divorced, Uncle Harvey's body was also brought back to Emory by their children and buried next to their mother.

Lorenza Robinson married Nina Johnson Robinson. They lived in Emory for a while but they spent many years living in Dallas. They later built a home in Emory and moved back. They became very active in the church when they returned to Emory. Uncle "Lor," as we called him, was known for his singing—especially in the male chorus. He was also a very good carpenter and painter. They are both deceased now. Their children are: Louise Robinson Calloway (deceased), Evelyn Robinson Coursey, Lorece Robinson (deceased), Lyndon Robinson, Douglas Robinson, and Wendell Robinson. My father was always very fond of Louise. He often spoke of how she sang her way through college (at Southwest Christian College in Terrell). When my father passed, she sang at his funeral. She usually would sing at the homecoming services at Prairie Grove each year.

Aunt Gletha Robinson Davis was married to A.L. Davis (deceased). However, we called him "Uncle Booger." Of all of my mother's sisters and brothers, I knew Aunt Gletha best. When I was growing up, we lived very close and I spent lots of time in and out of her house. Their children are: Bobbie Davis Cox, Bonnie Davis Clayton, and Eleanor Davis (Cunigan) Lipscomb. Eleanor and I were nearest in age, so we were very close during our childhood. We often played together and we also fought. I guess I never wanted her to boss me, even if she was older. But I guess that this is indicative of our closeness because siblings often fight. On the other hand, as an adult, I grew close to Bonnie (who still lives in Emory) and Bobbie (who lives in California). As you become adults, you don't think of age differences that much. Although I do not see any of these cousins on a regular basis, I still feel very close to all three of them. Aunt Gletha was always active in the community. And I always have had a close relationship with her. I often bought her birthday presents when buying my mother birthday presents. Their birthdays were very close. Unfortunately, Aunt Gletha has suffered from Alzheimer's for several years. She still resides in Emory. Her children have taken very good care of her during her illness. Bonnie is a Registered Nurse.

Choycie, the youngest male sibling, lived in California for many years. However, as a small child I can remember that he lived next door to us. I was very young, but I can remember that he used to make homemade hash. I can remember as a young child that I liked spicy food, and his hash was very spicy. Later as a young adult, I often visited Uncle Choyce (as we called him) in California. After retiring in California, Uncle Choyce moved back to Emory. I feel that this was a good move because he was able to be close to his family again. He had a chance to live near his sisters and brother again. If fact, he lived with my mother for a while. Uncle Choyce resided in Emory several years, but at the time of his death, he resided in a rehabilitation center in Sulphur Springs. He and my mother remained in close contact until the time of his death. I know that my mother really was glad to have him back in Texas, particularly since she doesn't like to fly. When my father was alive, my father, mother, and I made the trip to California several times (by car). Since his death I have been unable to get her to fly with me to California (or anywhere else). She flew once to see Aunt Loda just before her death but has had no desire to fly since.

Modis Robinson McMillan, my mother, is the youngest of the Robinson siblings. She was born in Emory on December 13, 1925. She doesn't know a lot about her history, but she says that she was told that she was born in a small house owned by "a white man." She doesn't know the circumstances, but she was told that her family had to move from this property when she was only two weeks old. Since her birthday is in December, my guess is that they probably moved during cold weather. My mother grew up in Emory; married my father in Emory; and (with the exception of moving about with my father in the United States Army to North Carolina) she has always lived there. For the most part, my mother has always been a housewife. She often worked as a housekeeper. She worked for Mrs. Louise Hood over a long period of time. When we were growing up, we were fortunate enough to enjoy homemade meals each day (including breakfast). We often had desserts during the week too. Because my father was a very high-profile individual, my mother was always a very low-key person. Other than church, and being supportive of my father in all of the school's activities, my mother was not active in the community. However, since all of her children have grown up and since the death of my father, my mother has become very active in the community. She is active in the church and in the community. I feel very proud when I see articles in the *Rains County Leader* with pictures of my mother being recognized for her work with the various civic organizations. My mother is an excellent mother, grandmother, great-grandmother, and great-great grandmother. The children of A.C. McMillan and Modis Robinson McMillan are: Alfred Clifton (named after my father) McMillan, Jewel Henry (named for both of his grandfathers) McMillan, Harold Dale McMillan, and me (their only daughter).

For several years, the Robinsons had a family reunion. This was an opportunity for the Robinsons to get together for fellowship and to get to know all of the families better. However, after about two or three attempts at making this an annual event, the reunion was discontinued.

Chapter 7
Making A Connection

When I was in high school, I was an officer in the New Homemakers of America (NHA). Before the schools were integrated, this was the equivalent to the (white) Future Homemakers of America. State meetings were held at Prairie View A&M College (now University). My father had often talked about our being related to the Registrar—Lemmon McMillan. During my sophomore year, I had the opportunity to meet Lemmon, Robert, and Sammie—the sons of Lemmon McMillan. This was the highlight of that meeting. They showed me around the campus and introduced me to their friends as their cousin. I never met their parents, but I really was happy to have met them.

Joseph McMillan, an educator, died after I moved to Dallas and became a teacher. I did not know him, but I did attend the funeral thinking that I might meet other McMillans—since my father was unable to attend the funeral. Later, a school in the Dallas Independent School District was named after him.

Then there was Ernest McMillan, who had established a name for himself during the civil rights movement as an outspoken young man that was in the news often for his participation in the Student

Non-Violent Coordinating Committee (SNCC, pronounced "Snick,"). Ernest was the son of Marion McMillan and Eva Partee McMillan. Marion was the son of Walter McMillan, a Dallas physician. He (Marion) attended the McMillan Reunion several times and knew my father quite well. Marion had a brother named Walter also. I never met their father, Dr. Walter McMillan, but his McMillan Sanitarium is still talked about today. It was completed in 1920 and Dr. McMillan practiced medicine there. At that time, such a facility in Dallas' Freedman's Town was considered "state of the art" for African Americans. His wife's name was Meirrell.

These were just some of the McMillans in my family's history that I was interested in knowing more about and eventually making the connection and learning how I am related to them. That is what the study of your genealogy is all about.

Chapter 8
A Legacy

The McMillans of Emory, Texas are indeed a legacy. The history of Rains County, if properly written, could not be written without their inclusion. There are many things that our family, the McMillans, will go down in history as being a part of the making of Rains County—Emory, Texas, specifically. One of the things that will cause future generations to be aware of the McMillans in Emory, Texas is that the street where I was born and where I spent my early childhood is now named McMillan Lane.

Desegregation of the Schools

In 1965, the Rains School District was desegregated. Even today, I often recall that first day. Even though Brown v Board of Education was the landmark Supreme Court Decision that should have meant that schools had to be desegregated; it did not happen in Rains County until 1965, after the Civil Rights Act of 1964. This was true for most of the area counties, although it was even later for others. Words cannot express those feelings when we arrived at Rains on the first day. I vividly remember our getting off the bus and entering the building.

I also remember how everyone stared as we entered. But there were no unwelcome remarks. Things went smoothly. Although I did not hear the statement, according to my best friend, Hella Mayberry, Mrs. Shiflet was standing in the hallways and said to some of her students (perhaps student council members), "a little nice breaks the ice." Of course, that was just like Mrs. Shiflet to make that kind of statement.

Some might not have been aware, but the year prior to the District's being desegregated, Kenneth McMillan had sought enrollment. However, in 1965, Kenneth and I were among the first group to enroll in Rains High School. Others in that first senior class were: Hella Mayberry (my best friend—then and now), Linda Givens, Darlene Hobbs, Bobby Kelly, and Glenn Turner (all of the Richland Community); Larry Robinson and Marcus Garrett (a grandson of Jewel McMillan) from Emory. We had all been classmates at St. Paul and had all grown up together in the Richland and Sand Flat Communities.

Our expectations of the school regarding our coming were probably more than what we witnessed upon our arrival. However, I am sure that their use of tokenism did contribute to our being as involved as we were. Kenneth and I made "Who's Who." I was the class treasurer and graduated third in my class. All of these were "firsts" for Rains High School and firsts for McMillans. I am sure that our teachers were amazed at the involvement of the "new" students at Rains. Even though I am emphasizing the involvement of the McMillans, the whole new group of students were quite involved—not just the senior class. Bobby Kelly, Glenn Turner, and Marcus Garrett were all great athletes, but so were some of the underclassmen at that time—Fred Hunter for one. He was probably the most athletic student at Rains— lettering in several sports. He also went on to play college basketball.

I became a member of the Beta Club (national honor society) and was, along with Linda Givens, nominated for homecoming queen. At that time, being nominated was a milestone. I was also a district UIL winner in shorthand and went on to the regional competition. I must admit, I did not know what shorthand was before attending Rains High School. That same year, Kenneth McMillan was named a class favorite. However, he was not pictured on the same photo with the white counterpart, as was the practice before we arrived. I guess that was a little too much to expect the first year.

After the first year, some of the other noted firsts were: Fannie Garrett (granddaughter of Jewel McMillan) made the Rainettes (the school drill team), Thomas "Tony" Garrett (grandson of Jewel McMillan) was an outstanding basketball player who also went on to play basketball in the military; and Jewel and Harold McMillan (my brothers) were all around students—lettering in sports and excelling academically as well. My older brother, Alfred, had been an outstanding student at St. Paul; but he never had the opportunity to attend Rains.

In 1967 my brother, Harold, was part of a pilot program that put Rains County's black and white elementary students together in the classroom for the first time. By 1968 the new countywide, all-levels comprehensive school was finished and everyone went to the same school.

Where we are today is the result of our upbringing and the influence it had on all we've done since. I contribute to my community and I am much like my parents and my ancestors who saw that education was the best way to improve the community.

A.C. McMillan, Principal

After 1965, many of the African American schools throughout Texas and the nation began closing. Many black teachers, and especially administrators, were left without jobs. When Sand Flat closed in 1969, my father, A. C. McMillan applied for the position of junior high principal at Rains Schools. Obviously, the Board realized that he was the best person for the job; and he was hired. Thus, my father became the first black principal in the history of Rains School, although he had been principal at Sand Flat for many years. And there has never been another African American principal since my father retired. He helped tremendously in the whole integration process of Sand Flat and Richland Schools becoming a part of the Rains Comprehensive School District. At that time, many of his friends and associates that had been his counterparts in many of the other small black schools were no longer principals. Several even worked under him as substitute teachers at Rains after they were no longer fully employed in their home districts. For the most part, there were only two black full-time teachers at Rains during his tenure there—Mrs. Bonnie Williams from Richland and Mrs. Thomas from Sulphur Springs. However, Mrs. Addine Thomas served as his secretary for several years and Mrs. Bonnie Clayton served as the school nurse. Mr. Bobbie Thomas served as the first Black to be elected to the school board. Later, Norris Lane and Anthony Porter also served on the school board.

After the death of my father in 1985, my brother, Harold McMillan, started a movement to rename the Rains Junior High School in the name of my father. This was met with opposition from some and much favor from others; however, the board voted this down. They suggested naming the library or another facility—but not the "school." Although the school was not renamed, the positive feelings for my father and his work in the school district were made known throughout the community. A number of individuals in the community voiced their support through "Letters to the Editor" in the *Rains County Leader.* One of those writing a letter in support of the renaming of the school was Mrs. Audie Shiflet, who had been my favorite teacher at Rains High School.

A. C. McMillan Scholarship

In 1986, through the efforts of the McMillan Family and Ruby Wade, The A. C. McMillan Scholarship was established to ensure that African American students at Rains High School received scholarships to continue their education after high school. Shajuana McMillan was the first scholarship recipient. Each year thereafter, scholarships have been awarded to deserving students. Although established to make it possible for African American students to receive scholarships, the scholarships have been awarded to deserving students of all races from both Emory and Point. For our family, one of the highlights of the spring graduation each year is the awarding of the A. C. McMillan Scholarship. I have presented this award at the graduation and so has Sylvia Lawe Williams (granddaughter of A. C. McMillan), Joe Jones, Jr. (nephew of A. C. McMillan) and Addine Thomas, his secretary and office clerk at Rains High School.

Community Leaders

My grandfather, Jewel McMillan, was probably one of the most respected leaders in the community African American Community. He was quite a philanthropist "back in the day." I can remember that once he was hospitalized in the Hopkins County Hospital in Sulphur Springs. He was so impressed with the nurses and the hospital that he donated land to the hospital district. In the same philanthropic spirit, I feel that many of the descendants of my grandfather (in their own way) continued to be leaders in the community.

As far as community activists, politicians, or law enforcers are concerned, our family also had some too. Aunt Mildred (Garrett), my father's sister, was the first African American to hold a political office in Rains County. She was on the city council and even served as the mayor pro tem. I can also remember that in the early 70s or late 60s my cousin, John L. Robinson, served as a sheriff's deputy. My father served on the Mental Health and Mental Retardation Board, the North East Texas Opportunity (NETO) Board, and often was the elections chair for the Sand Flat Community. Many programs that came to the community and to the school were through the efforts of my father. In the late 60s and early 70s, through the efforts of my father and others, many adults and youth were able to obtain jobs through the NETO or the NYC program. My uncle, Dave Garrett (husband of Mildred McMillan Garrett) also played an important role in NETO. My aunts, Annie Robinson (wife of my mother's brother Ozell) and Florene McMillan (wife of Elbert McMillan) played very vital roles in these community programs, particularly the senior meals program. Aunt Mildred Garrett worked with the senior meals program. Aunt Gletha Davis (my mother's sister) probably assisted more individuals in securing healthcare, food, shelter, and home improvements than any other individual in the community.

Civic Organizations

My father and uncle (Dave Garrett) were among the first African Americans to become members of the Lions Club, a national service organization for men. Both were honored as "Man of the Year" for that organization and both served as presidents. My brother, Alfred, also was a member of the Lion's Club. At present, those are the only family members that I know of that are or have been Lion's Club members.

My mother is quite involved in the community as well. She is a member of the Garden Club, which is a women's social club. Aunt Florene McMillan is also a member. I am not aware of others (relatives) that are members. My mother is also a member of the Economic

Development Committee and is involved in the work at the farmer's market. Along with coordinating the volunteers at the Museum, she is a member of the Rains County Genealogical Society and the Rains County Historical Association. Aunt Modean is very active with the Chamber of Commerce.

Most of my relatives are active in the church—either at Prairie Grove or at Jacksonville. At present, the ministers at Jacksonville are all relatives—Dwight Smith, Charles Smith, and Paul Smith (all sons of Lutishie McMillan). This is probably a first in our family—three brothers that are ministers at the same time and particularly at the same church. On the other hand, my husband has a history of ministers in his family—his father and grandfather were ministers.

Prairie Grove Baptist Church

Reverend H. L. Foster. My earliest memories of Prairie Grove Baptist Church are basically that Reverend H. L. Foster was the pastor. His wife, Artherine Lucy, was quite famous because of her integrating the University of Alabama back in the late 1950s. This drew national attention. I often heard that Autherine Lucy was Reverend Foster's wife; but at that time, I really was too young to know much about the Civil Rights Movement and its significance. In 2004, Reverend Foster returned to Emory as the speaker at the Annual Homecoming Services at Prairie Grove Baptist Church.

Reverend Cleveland Alexander. The next pastor, Reverend Cleveland Alexander, I remember well. Reverend Alexander is the minister that baptized me. At that time, baptisms were held in an outdoor pool. (I believe that it was near where the Collins lived at that time.) Reverend Alexander was my pastor from early childhood until I became an adult. He was the one that performed all of the marriages and funerals during my living in Emory. He also did the Eulogy at my father's funeral. He died shortly after my father's death. To date, there have been several ministers at Prairie Grove since Reverend Alexander—Reverend Richard Rollerson and Reverend W.R. Byrd are two of my favorites. Reverend Byrd, the current pastor, has instituted several programs in the community that make him stand out as "a man with much insight." Probably the thing that he has done that no other minister has is having services with the other churches in the community (Black and White) on special occasions—Christmas and Easter.

Musicians. As children, several of my cousins and I took music lessons from Mrs. A.J. Lewis in Lone Oak, Texas. Given the state of race relations in this country, this was quite a step toward progress. In the early 1960's, Mrs. Lewis taught African American children in her home—in fact, it was in her living room. We arrived on Saturday mornings and stayed all morning until all of us had completed our lesson. At the time, I think that each lesson was 30 minutes. I do not remember the cost for each lesson, but it was minimal—probably about a dollar. There were usually about four or five of us. Several years earlier, I had older cousins that had taken lessons in the same manner. So it was somewhat a tradition that we would all take lessons from Mrs. Lewis. Likewise, it was somewhat of a tradition to take music lessons on Saturday and then go on to Greenville to do shopping. Usually, one parent would drop us off at Mrs. Lewis' house, and another would pick us up—often enroute to Greenville to do shopping. If we went to Greenville with Aunt Deora, often she would buy Fannie new dresses. On a few occasions, I can remember that she also bought for me too.

Fannie (Garrett) and I were the church musicians for several years while Reverend Alexander was pastor. Fannie was a much better musician, but Reverend Alexander chose me as his musician. I often recall how when he would preach, he would call for "his musician" to come and play *"Just to Behold God's Face,"* and *"Something Within Me."* During those days, I often led songs too.

Just as Sand Flat played an important role in my development, so did Prairie Grove. Those lessons learned in Sunday school when taught by Mrs. Furiel Johnson and Mrs. Aline Randolph, are to be treasured. And who could forget Mrs. Furiel's hard work in preparing all those programs on special occasions such as Easter and Mother's Day. Cousin Lucille (Snell) always would sing *"Amazing Grace"* on Mother's Day. Then, there were the Board Meetings, Association Meetings, and the Congress. Fannie and I always looked forward to the Congress. Unlike today, no one stayed in hotels. Families opened their homes to the Congress delegates for the week. So Fannie and I looked forward to representing Prairie Grove. This gave us an opportunity to meet young people from other churches and to interact with other young people in the many programs of the Congress. I can remember our staying in Commerce, Sulphur Springs, Mt. Pleasant and Naples as delegates to the Congress.

Although I am older than Fannie, it seems that we generally did most things together. One summer we were hired by the church to paint the sign in front of the church. I cannot remember what we were paid; but whatever it was, I'm sure that it was a big addition to our salary as the musicians ($5 per Sunday together or $2.50 each).

While growing up in Emory and attending Prairie Grove, it was instilled in all of the young people in my family—and most others—the importance of the church. We always attended most of the programs of the church—Sunday school, training union (BTU), Vacation Bible School, etc. I always enjoyed most, but in our family, you went whether you enjoyed it or not. As a child, I used to tell my mother "when I grow up, no one would have to make me go to church; but I would not go to BTU." Unfortunately, the church that I attend doesn't have BTU.

95

However, I probably would have taken my daughter to BTU if we had it when she was growing up—just as I had been taken.

In 1971, when I moved to Dallas, I visited Memorial Missionary Baptist Church the first Sunday that I was away from home. I was a member for over 30 years. Yes, it was a lot like Prairie Grove—small membership and everyone knew all of the members by name. I am sure that is why I remained there for all of those years. However, I am now a member of the New Hope Baptist Church in Dallas, Texas. New Hope boasts that it is the "oldest African American witness" in Dallas.

Chapter 9
Education In Rains County
(Prior To 1965)

Sand Flat School

When I attended Sand Flat Elementary School (a Rosenwald School), it was for grades one through eight. Although, Sand Flat School is the only school that I remember in the Sand Flat community, before Sand Flat (in the late 1800's and early 1900's), African Americans attended the Henry's Chapel School. Fortunately when I grew up, students finishing the eighth grade were allowed to go on and complete high school at St. Paul High School (another Rosenwald School) in Greenville. Unfortunately, when my parents were growing up, the education of African Americans in Rains County usually ended at Sand Flat. Until 1951, students attending Sand Flat usually ended their education at the 10th grade. In 1951 St. Paul School agreed to accept the 11th grade students, thus allowing these students to attain a high school diploma. When I attended Sand Flat, it was for grades 1-8. Grades 9-12 went to St. Paul High School.

I often look back on my educational experience at Sand Flat

Elementary and St. Paul High School and compare that education with that of my mother's and father's. I really don't think that a lot changed. That is, when you consider the years involved. For example, when attending Sand Flat, many of our supplies and equipment for the school (if not all) came from Rains School (the white school) when they were finished with them. Our books, desks, etc. were all from Rains. I can remember one book in particular, *Little Black Sambo*. There were several copies of this book in our library. Whenever my father, who was the principal at the time, came across a copy of it, he would discard it immediately. He considered it degrading to African American children; and therefore, he refused to allow us to read it. He never allowed us to do things that he considered degrading. Other things that he tried to avoid our doing was eating in the back of restaurants or sitting in the balcony at movie theaters. Our family often went to Dallas to eat in black-owned restaurants and to see movies at black-owned/operated movie theaters. This way, we were able to sit in the front if we desired to do so and to see films that featured African American casts.

From 1954 – 1962, I attended Sand Flat School. Sand Flat was a small (three classroom) building in which much teaching and a lot of learning took place.

I can also remember that when I entered first grade, Mrs. Doris Robinson (Washington) was my teacher. She was married to my mother's brother, Choycie Robinson. She taught first through third grade in the same room. I liked this because I could often do the work of the second and third grade and sometimes she combined the work and all had classes together. She was really a good teacher. We might have had second-hand books, desks, etc. but the education gained was definitely first class.

During this time, Mrs. Teresa Maples (Carraway) was the teacher of the fourth through the sixth grade. For a short period after Mrs. Maples left, Mrs. Bonnie Williams, from Point (Richland) was my teacher. She was the wife of my father's close friend—Mr. Cleveland Williams, Jr. Mrs. Maples, as well as Mrs. Williams, were excellent teachers also.

By the time that I reached the seventh grade (which is now called junior high or middle school), my father was my teacher. He taught seventh and eighth grades, along with being principal, coach, bus driver, cook, father and mentor. He was related to most of the students. I called him "Daddy," and most of the other students called him "Uncle A.C." instead of Mr. McMillan, although there were some that did call him Mr. McMillan. Whatever name was used, all students were treated equally. This often resulted in everyone's being punished when the classes were noisy, etc.

During this time period, there were no indoor restrooms, which was probably typical of many rural schools (even the white schools). However, as time passed and the white schools were improved, Sand Flat and most other African American schools did not progress at the same rate. Although during the time that I first attended Sand Flat we did not have indoor restrooms, telephones, government lunch program, or school bus, we did get indoor restrooms, telephones, a school milk program, and a real "school bus" was purchased during the time that I attended. These were all real milestones for Sand Flat. I witnessed many history-making events.

There are many fond memories of this time period. I can remember the school plays, and many wonderful experiences that we had while at Sand Flat.

A Typical Day at Sand Flat (when I attended)

Classes started promptly with the singing of a patriotic song— "The Star Spangled Banner," "America," "America the Beautiful," or

"The Battle Hymn of the Republic." There was always a prayer and the "Pledge of Allegiance." All students were prepared to lead the prayer, Pledge, etc. Students spent very little time off task. Often assignments were combined for more than one class. This was an excellent opportunity to learn more than the assignments in your books. For example, if you were in the fourth grade, you could do the fifth grade math, etc.

Some of the duties that students might have been assigned include: helping in the lunchroom (sweeping, washing dishes); sweeping the classrooms, hallways, or the porch; erasing the chalkboards and cleaning the erasers; and occasionally students were allowed to ring the bell. Students were taught to never walk past paper on the floor—no matter whether you dropped it or not. You were to pick it up. I can recall my father's placing a dollar bill in wadded up paper to see who would pick it up. The lucky student would be rewarded by being able to keep the money.

Personal hygiene and appearance were also very important. Students were not allowed to wear clothing that was viewed as unacceptable by the principal or the teachers. These opinions and decisions were final. There was no appeal process.

Looking back, I now realize even more what wonderful teachers we had at Sand Flat. Their creativity was immeasurable. They were exemplary by anyone's standards.

We always looked forward to "recess," better known today as "a break." There was a morning recess and an afternoon recess. There was only one lunch period, so all students and teachers ate at the same time. Lunchtime was a very interesting time. Many students brought their own lunch and some ate in the lunchroom. My brothers and I, however, always ate in the lunchroom. I even remember helping to prepare the lunches, which were prepared by either one of the teachers or my father. I think they probably took turns. These lunches included tuna salad sandwiches, or my father's own recipe for making bologna, pressed ham, or hot links taste like a "gourmet" sandwich. This sandwich (at a cost of $.15) was the lunch. You could add a package of chips and/or a soft drink for an additional amount. There were also cookies, peanuts, and candy bars that could be purchased in the lunchroom. I sometimes think of those days when I see a "Tom's" truck today. Once the school milk program was started, everybody (and I do mean everybody) was required to have milk with lunch. Of course this was a real addition to the lunch program at our school.

After lunch, of course we would continue with our classes. I often look back and wonder how those teachers could keep up with where they left off when teaching so many classes. Somehow, though, we would pick up where we left off before lunch. Sometimes we would have to wait for a short period for the teacher to finish seeing to it that the lunchroom had been cleaned before returning to class. Classes were always orderly, even if the teacher was not present. And it was a real honor if my father allowed you to ring the hand-held bell. Because my father was the principal—and often I served as his secretary—I knew a few little known facts that other students probably were not privy to. For example, the bell at Sand Flat always rang about 10 minutes early because the clocks were set ahead of time. My father called that "Sand Flat Time." The reason for this was so that the teachers could go to the bank after school and would not have to leave early. (It also meant arriving minutes early.) At 3:00 (Sand Flat Time) the school day ended. The students who lived in Jacksonville would ride the bus and the students who lived within two miles would have to walk. Of course that was when the bus was actually a truck with a camper on the back or a panel truck with seats in the back. Later, after the purchase of the "yellow school bus" all students were able to ride the bus.

There are many other fond memories of this time period. I can remember the school closing plays, Christmas plays, and many wonderful experiences that we had while at Sand Flat. Sometimes I still hear expressions that remind me of those plays or I remember songs that Eleanor and I played on the piano ("Up on the Rooftop") for the Christmas programs. I can remember going to spend the weekend with Mrs. Robinson (in Winnsboro, Texas) and spending the weekend with Mrs. Maples in Henderson, Texas. Her daughter, Valeria, and I were very good friends. I can remember participating in the "League" reciting the poem, "O Captain, My Captain." Later, when I attended the desegregated schools, I learned that "League" was actually the University Interscholastic League. At that time, however, there was a different one for us. Instead of the state meetings being in Austin, they were at Prairie View College (now Prairie View A & M University). Because my father was the principal, I can remember traveling to the league in various cities to see Sand Flat students participate. Usually the students participating were from the Hunter family and the Jackson family. Edwin Collins was also quite an athlete. (But that was before my time.) I can also remember playing basketball. Although I made the team, it was probably because of a lack of students to choose from. I can remember playing in various towns as my father coached us. He was also the track coach (and for whatever else Sand Flat students were participants). And let's not forget that he was also the bus driver to all of these events, as well as the driver for the bus on a daily basis. And then there were the fundraisers—I guess today we would call them "Classics"—when my father arranged for Norris High School (from Commerce) to play against Brownsboro "LaRue" High School. At the time, Joe Jones, Jr., my cousin, was the coach of

LaRue High School. These were two of the best basketball teams in the area, so this was quite exciting. This event was held at the Rains High School gym. Actually, this was the only time that I had ever gone to anything at Rains High School before attending in 1965.

Some of the most memorable trips that were taken by the school were: Wonder Cave (in San Marcos), The Alamo (in San Antonio), The State Capitol, The Sam Rayburn Library (in Bonham), The Dallas Zoo, Mrs. Baird's Bakery, a radio station (KNOK with Jimmy Avant) in Dallas, a train ride from Mineola to Dallas, and a trip to Mexico. The train ride was memorable because many of the students (and parents) from Sand Flat and Richland had not been on a train before. That is, most of them had not. The trip to Mexico was most memorable because not only did we actually leave the United States, we had our first opportunity to sleep overnight in a motel. (I still remember the motel was the Chariot Inn in Austin.) I later stayed there as an adult. It wasn't the same! My father had allowed my friend from St. Paul, Valarie Tarver, to go along with me. Since I was in high school at the time, it was good having an older friend along.

Although it was not a school field trip, I can remember my father's letting me along with my brother "Chief" go with him to Austin to pick up the school's first school bus. Previously, several different vehicles (of my father's)—a panel truck and a pickup with a cover—had served as the "bus." I can remember that Edwin Collins went along to drive our car back and Cousin Ethel Murray also went along. This was an exciting trip because we got to eat out at several restaurants, visit the State Capitol Building in Austin and to take pictures of the memorable event.

There were other things that made Sand Flat special. For instance, the graduations were very special. Because I was my father's "secretary," I actually wrote out the "Perfect Attendance" awards and the "Diplomas." I even wrote out my own. I can recall my own graduation, which included students from Sand Flat and Richland. All girls wore black or navy skirts with white blouses. The ceremonies were at Prairie Grove Baptist Church and the Superintendent would always attend. At the time of my graduation, the Superintendent was Mrs. Margarite Braziel. I can still remember how I always hated to hear her refer to my father as "A.C." when he would introduce her as "Mrs. Braziel." I felt that she should have responded, "Thank you, Mr. McMillan." It was always "A.C." However, now that I have grown older, I do realize that the Anglos are not as formal as African Americans at such ceremonies. So, I might have been misreading the superintendent's intent.

That year, not only did we have a graduation, we had an eighth grade prom. We had an opportunity to dress up (semi-formally) and to dance. There weren't many occasions for us to dance, and there were none where we were to dress semi-formal. We had a "hifi" (a record player) and plenty 45s (records) to play. Since none of us were dating, we were all brought by our parents. This was a very exciting event because students from several surrounding communities were also invited.

Sand Flat did not have a government lunch program as most schools now have, but we did have delicious food. As I mentioned earlier, I can remember the teachers, along with my father, preparing the daily lunches. However, on holidays, other parents would assist and we would have the traditional Thanksgiving and Christmas meals. I am not sure who purchased the food, but there was always plenty of it. I guess when speaking of the lunchroom, as I mentioned earlier, we did not have the school lunch program, but we did have the school milk program. In order to have it, a certain number of students had to drink milk each day. You guessed it! My father required all students to participate in this program—whether you liked milk or not. Unfortunately, I did not. However, as I grew older and more sophisticated, I learned that I am lactose intolerant. That explains why I always had difficulty drinking the milk and would get sick to my stomach.

Not only did my father enable Sand Flat School to receive the milk program, but also it was through his efforts that the Richland School was able to get the milk program. I am sure that he worked closely with Mr. Wesley, the principal at Richland, on this project just as he did on many others.

The Role of St. Paul High School

As I stated earlier, when students graduated from eighth grade at Sand Flat Elementary School (even with a class ring), they then went on to St. Paul High School, which was another Rosenwald School. When I think about the Civil Rights Movement, and how the plight of Blacks in America changed by integration or the desegregation of the schools, I know first hand that this had to be one of the biggest improvements to the education process for individuals in Rains County and the other counties that sent students to St. Paul High School. That is not to say that attending St. Paul was all bad, because given our circumstances, it was the best that we could do at the time. If not for St. Paul, I would have had to move away from home to complete high school. Thank God, this inequity ended with my generation.

When I attended St. Paul High School (1962-65) the conditions were so bad that when I recall some of my experiences it seems as though it was almost a century ago. I can remember leaving home each day around 7:00 a.m. and not returning until about 5:00 p.m. This was on a good day when there were no problems. However, I can also remember arriving at school as late as noon and returning home from school after 7:00 p.m. If there were ever problems with the bus, we would have to wait for a bus to come from another long bus route to pick us up to take us to school. We had to stay on a sometimes very hot bus or a very cold bus to wait for another bus to come. I can also remember missing the bus and my mother taking me to catch up with the bus. Even under such circumstances, I sometimes managed to have perfect attendance and to always be an "A" student. I also must mention that during those days, our building (which, by today's standards) would have been condemned for use as a school, and probably for anything else. A few years ago, I mentioned to my mother that there were many days that I did not attend classes because when it was cold, we were allowed to go to the rooms where it was warm. (All rooms were heated by wood heaters.) Then there were the days that I spent all day typing in the Principal's Office. Because of understaffing, students with typing skills were often used to type in the office. I can especially remember helping the secretary, Mrs. Mattie Vaughn. Mrs. Vaughn and her husband (Johnny Vaughn) lived in Emory for a while. Mr. Vaughn drove the St. Paul school bus. At this time Mr. D. White was the principal. I can also remember typing for teachers, i.e., Mr. Cleveland Williams, Mr. Odell Standifer, and Mr. Willie Brown.

Extracurricular Activities. Students at St. Paul High School were also denied having the extracurricular activities to participate in because of the lack of funds and lack of personnel. Transportation was also a factor, since the school was not in the neighborhood. However, students at St. Paul had pride in themselves and in their school. Their families were very supportive of the school and school activities. We did not have a band, or a football team; but we had one of the best choirs in the area. I can remember being in the choir and traveling with the choir. We had girls' and boys' basketball teams. I played on the basketball team during my junior year. I lettered; but we did not get letter jackets. However, there were times that the teams did receive letter jackets. I am not sure why we never got ours.

I guess some of the fondest memories of extracurricular activities would be of Mrs. Lucy Mae Thrash, the homemaking teacher, who put on the fashion show. In her homemaking classes, you would make an outfit (to her specifications, of course) and would wear it in the fashion show. She also sponsored the N.H.A. (New Homemakers of America). I was a participant each of the three years that I attended St. Paul. Through this organization we took an annual trip to Prairie View A & M University to participate in the State meeting. I was an Area Officer, so I also participated in the area meetings. I can remember traveling with Mrs. Thrash to Hamilton Park High School in Richardson for the area meeting when I ran for and received the office of treasurer. I can remember the area meeting the next year being at Texas College in Tyler. This meeting was somewhat sad because we knew that St. Paul was closing and this would be our last year to participate in the N.H.A. In fact, I think that it might have been the last year for the N.H.A. There was also an area Christmas Party in Dallas at the Convention Center. We attended by bus. This was very exciting because it was in Dallas and we dressed semi-formal. Mrs. Thrash and Mr. Williams were two of the best teachers that I knew at St. Paul because they involved the students in the youth organizations for homemaking and agriculture, although I was not that interested in being a "homemaker." But I did earn the "Crisco Award" for homemaker of the year. Those experiences—meetings and competitions—were priceless.

School Plays, Talent Shows, Etc. Mrs. Evelyn Franklin and Mrs. Lexie Mallard were also teachers for whom I have fond memories. Mrs. Franklin taught English and Mrs. Mallard taught social studies. I can remember that Mrs. Mallard would sing on the assembly programs and talent shows. Mrs. Franklin conducted our class play as juniors. I cannot remember the name of the play, but I can remember how diligently she worked with us to put on the play. I can remember that several of us had lengthy parts and did not remember our lines. Since the scene was sitting around in a living room, we placed our scripts inside magazines so that we could read our lines. I can also remember a physical education teacher from Tyler, Texas (Ms. Burton). She had us do a version of the "Nutcracker" ballet as a part of a Christmas program. These were some of the special programs that we had at St. Paul. However, each Friday, we had assembly programs where the various classes were allowed to be responsible for doing the program. This was an opportunity to appear on program before the entire student body. These programs would always begin with a song, scripture, and prayer. Often Psalms 100 would be repeated in unison along with the Pledge of Allegiance to the Flag and the Lord's Prayer. (During that time, these same procedures would take place in homeroom on a daily basis.) Of course, it was soon not permissible for the Lord's Prayer or scriptures to be repeated in the classroom.

Friends. One day, while visiting with my mother, I looked through a scrapbook that I had compiled when I was in high school. One of the things that I was really surprised to see was a list of my classmates, my friends. I included these names because I would never have remembered all of them otherwise. These are the names on that list:

Girls

- Ruby Kay Brown
- Dollie Nelson
- Rachel Reed
- Mary Lou Evans
- Lena Ramsire

- Lola Ramsire
- Judy Williams
- Dessie Armstrong
- Minnie Wilson
- Roynell Wilson
- Sheryl Cooksie
- Freda Loftin
- Beverly Herron
- Tippie Drennon
- Elean Murphy
- Easter Ford
- Docery Whetstone
- Elsie Fridie
- Lauretta Miles
- Anna Dean Miles
- Hella Mayberry
- Laverla Thrash
- Erma Joyce Lee
- Darlene Hobbs
- Linda Givens
- Valarie Tarver

Males

- Willie Vation
- Leon Madkins
- Lonnie Horton
- Kenneth McMillan
- Larry Robinson
- Marcus Garrett
- Joe Frank Hale
- Willie Rhoden

- Bobby Kelly
- Glen Turner
- Sidney Johnson
- James Fry
- Ezell Boyd
- Clarence (C.L.) Reed

Among my best friends were Hella Mayberry, Anna Dean Miles, Laverla Thrash ("Rushie"), Valarie Tarver, Erma Joyce Lee ("Pete"), Sheryl Cooksie, Linda Givens, Darlene Hobbs, Ruby Kay Brown, and Lauretta Miles. I have not been in touch with Valarie or Lauretta for many years. Pete lives in Los Angeles, California. I have visited her there and she used to call me when she would come to Texas. Rushie lives in Dallas, and because we are relatives, I see her at family gatherings—funerals, weddings, etc. Anna Dean married Cletis Johnson from Sulphur Springs. She lives there now. Like Rushie, I see Anna Dean at funerals, etc. in Emory. Ruby Kay lived out of state for a number of years, but she moved back to Texas several years ago. So I occasionally hear from her through Hella or Lois. Hella, Darlene, and Linda all went to Rains and were a part of my graduation class. Even though they are from Point, I am not in contact with Linda or Darlene. On the other hand, Hella and I have remained best friends since childhood. Even in college when we were at two different institutions, we remained best friends. In fact, today, we are "family." My daughter and grandchildren call her "Aunt Helen" and her nieces (Lois Hoskins Lane's daughters) call me "Aunt Gwen."

Chapter 10
Transitions

Segregated Public Facilities

Growing up as an African American in Emory, Texas during the 1950's and 1960's was a very interesting time—not only in Rains County—but it was an interesting time in the history of the United States of America. It was impossible for me (and my friends, brothers, classmates, etc.) to not be listed as "one of the firsts" on someone's list. Just as Dr. Martin Luther King, Jr. had dreams for his children ("that someday they would not be judged by the color of their skin, but by the content of their character"), I had dreams for myself, for my family, and for the children that I would have someday. I looked forward to the day that it would not be a notable event to be the "first" in otherwise ordinary day-to-day activities for my Anglo American peers.

My father was an educator for many years in Emory. As a child, my being an educator (teacher) was the furthest thing from my mind. This just goes to show the impact that parents have on us—in spite of ourselves. I, like many girls in my age group, thought of being a nurse or a secretary. Other than those two careers, I really did not spend a lot of time thinking about beyond college. My father, older brother, and most of my relatives had attended Texas College in Tyler, Texas. For example Ruby Jo Jackson (Wade), Joe Jones, Jr., Telesta Jones (Riggs), Alton Ray Jones, Tredis Jones (Griffin), Emma McMillan (Madlock), Juanita McMillan (Briggs), Patricia Jackson (Jackson), Bobbie Davis (Jackson Cox), and my brother Alfred attended Texas College while I was still in elementary and high school. Later on, I can remember that Patricia Hobbs (Loyd) went to Jarvis Christian College in Hawkins, Texas along with Maude Ruth Turner from Point. At the same time, Patricia's sister Anna Hobbs (Stokes) had attended Bishop College in Marshall, Texas. Luverta Hunter, on the other hand had attended Bishop College in Dallas, Texas. But Texas College remained the favorite choice of African Americans from Emory graduating from St. Paul. I think that was because of my father's influence.

My parents had always instilled in us that we were not inferior and that no one could make us feel inferior unless we let them. Likewise, we were always reminded that others were just as good as we were; we were not superior. All individuals should be treated equally.

However, this was a time when all public facilities throughout the south were segregated, that included our neighborhoods as well. Therefore, there was not a lot of direct interaction with individuals of different races or religions. Since these were the existing conditions when I grew up, I only had African American friends and that seemed perfectly normal to me. I didn't give a lot of thought to it ever being any other way. However, I do remember that when I first heard the news that African Americans would be allowed to use all public accommodations, I did not realize that it meant "some day." Therefore, when a few of my friends (cousins) and I got the news, we went to the Drum Stick (a walk-up restaurant, similar to the Dairy Queens at that time) and tried to place an order. There was a man named Lloyd McKinney that turned us back by telling us that we could not be served there. Imagine, we only wanted to place a to-go order at a window. I never was brave enough to test the system again until years later!

Desegregation of Schools

In the fall of 1964 while I was a student at St. Paul High School, I was one of the many students in our school, as well as similar schools throughout the south, that was informed that next year, we would not be attending St. Paul. However, we were not told where we would be attending school the 1965 - 1966 school year. This was a time of uncertainty for us. It was especially difficult for me and for my class because it meant not knowing where we would spend senior year—or more specifically, where we would graduate. However, as the school year continued, students from various surrounding communities were informed where they would be. For example, since Commerce had annexed St. Paul, the students from the St. Paul (Neylandville) community would be attending Commerce High School. But some time passed before we learned that we would be attending the Rains High School in Emory, Texas. We would no longer be bused from Emory to rural Hunt County in order to graduate from high school. Since Sand Flat was an elementary school, students in the elementary grades (1-8) would still be attending Sand Flat. Only the high school students would be attending Rains. Although the landmark civil rights case, Brown v The Board of Education of Topeka, Kansas, had been passed in 1954, to my knowledge there had been no changes in Emory or even the state of Texas, until 1965, which was 11 years later. But now, at last, I would be a part of "the first" African American students to attend Rains High School and in "the first" graduating class. At the time, I really did not understand the significant role that these two things would be in the history of Rains County and Rains High School in particular.

After the closing of St. Paul High School and my becoming a senior at Rains High School, my visions of attending college began to change. For the first time in my life, I began looking at previously "all white" institutions as possibilities. Before this, I had only considered Historically Black Colleges and Universities (HBCUs). Attending Rains opened my eyes to many opportunities that I had not previously been afforded, but there were also many negatives in graduating from a school that you only attended the senior year. I am sure that my St. Paul classmates that attended schools in Commerce, Wolf City, Caddo Mills, Lone Oak, Greenville, Celeste, etc. also shared these feelings. We were somewhat displaced. I feel that the transition from St. Paul High School to Rains High School was very smooth. Although when I see the movie or newsreels depicting the desegregation of Central High School in Little Rock, Arkansas, I still can identify with the students unloading the bus on that first day. My brother, Jewel (Chief), and I decided to ride the bus along with the other students on the first day so that we would arrive with everyone else. Even though, there are a lot of things that I do not remember, I can remember some things from that day quite vividly. My father had been the bus driver for Sand Flat School. On that day, however, he was the driver for Richland and Sand Flat. My brother and I did not live the required two miles to qualify for riding the bus, but everyone rode the bus the first day. I remember that when we got off the bus we all walked inside of the building together. We did not know where we were going—we just kept walking.

Although I was young during the Civil Rights Movement of the 1960's, I do recall having watched the desegregation of Central High School in Little Rock, Arkansas on the television. And I can remember my father following all of the events on television, in the newspapers, and in *Jet* and *Ebony* magazines. For African Americans in this time period, *Jet* and *Ebony* were the two main sources for keeping up with current events in the African American communities throughout the country. My father took the *Post Tribune* (an African American newspaper published in Dallas) and the *Kansas City Call*. But no source of information was as detailed as the *Jet* and *Ebony*.

It was apparent that the entire community had all kinds of perceptions of how we were to be prepared for this monumental step in the education of African Americans in Emory, Texas. The African American community was probably just as skeptical as the white community.

I guess that the Anglo students were just as apprehensive as we were. After all, it was a new experience for them also. And I am certain that their parents were even more apprehensive than they were. My father often spoke of the comments that he got from other parents (Anglo) before and after we entered Rains. He told us that he assured them that he was just as concerned about the impact on "his" daughter as they were about theirs. He also assured them that their children were "just as good as I was."

I am sure that there were many meetings that took place in the Anglo community in preparation for our coming. The meeting that I can recall in the Sand Flat community was held at the Prairie Grove Baptist Church. The superintendent at the time came out and spoke to the African American parents about Rains High School. The thing that I remember most is that he explained that we could not be in the drill team (The Rainettes) the first year. Somehow, he seemed to feel that was important to us. On the other hand, I think that was not high on our list of priorities. After all, we did not know (or care about) the Rainettes at that point. We were more concerned about our classes and the new teachers that we would have. We were concerned as to whether the curriculum would be the same as at St. Paul. (It was not.) We had not had the variety of advanced courses, electives, or extra-curricular activities. We learned that our new school welcomed our African American young men to join the football team, basketball team, tennis team, and baseball team, etc. This seemed somewhat odd, since we were advised that young ladies would not be able to participate in the drill team nor the cheerleaders our first year. Not having had a drill team, football team, or cheerleaders our last few years at St. Paul we had not even considered being in these organizations—at least I had not. But somehow being told that I could not just did not seem fair. Usually, the U.I.L. rule that applied for athletics also applied for cheerleaders and drill team.

However, to the surprise of the Rains High School staff, they learned that some of the expectations (or requirements) were lower at Rains than they had been at St. Paul. An example of this was the number of credits for graduation. Because we had not had study halls at St. Paul and our schedules had been a full day of classes, in most cases, we had more credits than the students that were our counterparts at Rains. I had enough credits to graduate from high school when I arrived at Rains.

As a student at Rains High School, I was elected to "Who's Who." I was senior class treasurer, a member of the Beta Club (the honor society), the choir, and a participant and winner in the University Interscholastic League (U.I.L.) in shorthand. For the record, these were all "firsts."

In many ways, I often felt that the white teachers at Rains discriminated against the African American students—in many cases, without being aware that they were doing so. At other times, they overcompensated to make us feel that we were a part of the whole school. An example of this was the senior play. When the parts were given for the senior play, I recall being the only African American that was given a part. However, in order that more African Americans were included, the teacher, Mrs. Constance Griffin, wrote in an additional scene that included an African American family. In my opinion and that of my classmates, this was not necessary.

Attending Rains High School in this first group to desegregate the school district was probably a much easier task for the students (white and black) than it was for their parents, the teachers, administrators, and the school board members. Even though we were the ones that would be attending school, we probably did not have to make as many mental adjustments as our parents had to make. At the time, my father, who was the principal of the Sand Flat School, was credited as being the individual that was responsible for the smooth transition of the whole desegregation process in Rains County. Although I do believe that he played a major role, I do know that a lot of the responsibility was also placed on the parents of the students involved, the administration, and especially the students. Although we had never really been in this type of situation before, we were the ones that had to prepare for this big change. The students at Rains could probably be described as "curious" as much as anything else. I don't know what their real feelings were toward us, but I do not recall any situations that indicated that they did not welcome our presence.

We came from a school that used letter grades (A-F). Rains used numbers such as 50-100. I found it hard to understand how they could determine what weight to give an "A." As I stated earlier, we also came from a school where we always had a full class load. Therefore, we had more credits than were needed when graduation time came. In fact, when I entered Rains, I only needed about one course to graduate; but I still took a full schedule of classes. I do not think that I had a choice.

I tried to take full advantage of all of the opportunities that attending this school had afforded me. I sang in the choir and really excelled in shorthand and typing. I was a member of the Beta Club, Who's Who, and was class treasurer. I also attended all athletic events, field trips, etc. I can remember attending a dinner with the Spanish Club in Greenville, and I was not a member of that club. Mrs. Shiflet was the sponsor and she invited me to attend. I had never eaten at that restaurant (El Sombrero) or any other Mexican restaurant before, so it was an excellent opportunity for me to eat there.

Overall, integration/desegregation went well for all involved. I can only remember a few times that I was not comfortable with situations that were racial. Once in the auditorium a student, Rene Lankford, was describing someone as having "a nigger nose." As a teenager I was quite uncomfortable with this (and so was Rene, when she realized that I heard her). Another time there was a discussion about interracial dating. Some of the Anglos did not approve based on religion. But I guess the three incidents that I remember most involved senior activities. When the actors were cast for the senior play (I mentioned this earlier.), the sponsor (Mrs. Constance Griffin) wrote in parts for the African American students. Perhaps the intent was good, but we did not like the idea. The second event was when an African American (Kenneth McMillan) was chosen as a class favorite along with an Anglo (Claudette Varnon) and they were not allowed to pose on the same picture. And third, when we had the senior prom, students could not invite anyone other than Rains students. This might have always been the rule, but somehow we felt that it was for us. Thus, there were only a few actual "couples" that attended. My best friend Hella Mayberry and I went with my cousin, Marcus Garrett. Gwendolyn Johnson (from Point) also went with us. Fortunately, the senior football players nominated homecoming contestants for queen.

Glenda Givens (from Point) and I were nominated. The only votes that we received might have been those from the persons that nominated us—but we were nominated!

Another incident that happened during our senior year was that some of us found notes in some of the textbooks to parents that had been sent out the year prior to our arrival. These notes were warning the parents that there were students at Rains that had lice. Whew! We were really glad that the lice were discovered before we arrived. We probably would have been accused of bringing lice with us. In fact, it was at Rains that I learned about head lice. I am not sure of the reason, but African American children do not generally have lice. But I am not sure that the faculty, teachers, and parents at Rains knew that. Therefore, we were relieved that they had it prior to our arrival.

The Desegregation of Facilities

Just as the Supreme Court Decision Brown v Board meant that the schools throughout the south would now be desegregated, and the Civil Rights Act of 1964 meant that other such facilities as restaurants, hotels, and all other such facilities would now be open to us as well. However, in Emory there were not many facilities to test this freedom. Next to attending the segregated schools and having to change to the what had been an "all white" school district, the next biggest change was to be able to enter the front door of any and all facilities that had once denied our entering through the front door or denied our admittance altogether. One of the ways that this was made easier is that through the integration of the schools, students were often acting on behalf of the school in traveling to games, field trips, or competitions. This enabled the African American students to be able to experience many activities that they had not even thought of before. For example, when the basketball team played games that were out-of-town, students often were among those stopping at such places as Dairy Queen for food or refreshment after games. The senior class went bowling in Tyler, went to the movies in Dallas, and had a junior/senior prom at a hotel in Sulphur Springs. Mrs. Shiflet invited all of her students to attend the Spanish Club's party at a Mexican restaurant in Greenville. (Prior to this, my only experience eating Mexican food was through TV dinners.) All of these were completely new experiences for my fellow African American classmates and me; but we made the adjustment easily, even though all of the African Americans did not participate in all of these activities. I, on the other hand, was eager to attend all senior functions. Since being a senior was also a new experience, I was not aware of the many senior activities that students at Rains were able to be a part of. During the spring semester, I received an invitation to attend a graduation tea for Claudette Varnon, one of my new friends and classmates. Although this was the only invitation that I received, I overheard (probably by accident) that a number of my classmates' parents had various kinds of graduation parties for them. However, Claudette's was the only one that I received an invitation. I have always had a special place in my heart for her and for her mother because of my being invited to this event. This was the first time that I had ever been to a tea—Claudette's Mother-Daughter Tea.

Having been in Mrs. Shiflet's shorthand class was also a very positive opportunity for me. Because of Mrs. Shiflet's being a teacher of seniors, and because her son, David, was in our shorthand class, I recall her having a Christmas party for our class at her house, which was just a few minutes' walk from the school. On another occasion, I was invited to a party at her house that was held for the basketball team. (My brother, Chief, was on the team.) This relationship with Mrs. Shiflet had the biggest impact on my career choice. I admired her so much that I wanted to be a business teacher just like Mrs. Shiflet.

(Before attending Rains, I thought that being a teacher would be the last thing that I would want to be.)

I think that perhaps one of the things that white Americans feared was that once facilities were desegregated, African Americans would want to be involved in all of the day-to-day activities that the whites had always been the only ones to enjoy. Some had the preconceived notion that one of the immediate differences would be that African Americans would want to attend their churches and African American young men would now be able to marry their daughters. In fact, some parents feared even having their daughters attending the same schools as African American students. Ironically, some African American parents had these same biases. Many parents feared for their children even attending the "white schools." Some feared for different reasons. One common fear was that African American males would start dating the white female students (or would be perceived as doing so) and this might put their lives in danger. However, I must say these were the extremes. For my household, none of the previous mentioned preconceived notions existed. We chose to concentrate on the real issue—getting an education for my brothers and for me.

Education after Rains High School

After attending Rains, I attended Henderson County Junior College (now Trinity Valley Community College). However, I thought that I would be attending Prairie View College with friends—Hella Mayberry, Laverla Thrash, and Valarie Tarver. Hella's sister, Lois Hoskins (Lane) was already attending Prairie View. Much to my surprise, the recruiters from Henderson County Junior College (now Trinity Valley Community College) did such good job of recruitment— even met with my parents at my home—my father was sold on that being the best place for me. At Henderson County I can remember the first days—maybe weeks—as being miserable. I had made adjustments before so this was just another challenge. Fortunately, I had my cousins Marcus Garrett, David Garrett, Troy and Kenneth McMillan, along with Bobby Kelly (from Point) and Richard Griffis (from Greenville). Of course, this caused many students to wonder why I traveled with my own male entourage. Finally, I accepted the idea, adjusted, made friends, and eventually learned to love "HCJC." (We called it Hick Jick.)

Since this institution had not had African Americans very long either, it was very similar to going to Rains, however, racial prejudices were a little more pronounced. Again, the African American athletes were welcomed—particular such football stars as Johnny Davis, Margene Adkins, Louis Scott, and basketball player Lonnell Galloway. At least two of these athletes went on to play football at major universities and later played professional football. But the drill team and cheerleaders remained white for a number of years. Since this was a time of unrest on campus and throughout the country with the assassination of Dr. Martin Luther King, Jr., it was also a time when African American students became aware of the need to organize and make our issues known. I guess that the biggest display of our being able to come together for a purpose was the memorial ceremony on campus in honor of Dr. King. A young minister from Dallas, Millard Elder, was very instrumental in our having this program which took place in the auditorium.

East Texas State University

Later, after graduating from Henderson County, I attended East Texas State University. At the time that I graduated from HCJC, my brother (Jewel) was also graduating from Rains High School. Once again, the decision was made by my father as to where I should continue my education. Economically, it was best that my brother and

I attend East Texas State University (now Texas A & M University-Commerce). Although it was not my decision, it was a good one.

At ETSU, the adjustment was easy. Many of my friends from HCJC had transferred to ETSU. I met new friends—some became friends for life—Vivian Bradshaw and Dorothy Barns, along with Frank and Jesse Jordan, Ida Nunn (Coleman) Marion Willard, and Rita Lincoln (Cloman), for example. Although the school had been desegregated for several years, there were still many "firsts" for African Americans while I attended. This continued to be a time of firsts for African American students. This was truly a time of transition. This was immediately following the silent protest at the 1968 Summer Olympics. During this time Ernest McMillan, a Black Activist in Dallas, was constantly in the news as protests and demonstrations for the equal rights of African Americans were staged throughout the country. At this time, there were no African American organizations on campus. Again, I found myself in the middle of the African American female movement to get African American sororities on campus. I had never been interested in being in a sorority. In fact, I never really understood why anyone would. I considered myself too much of an "individual" to be a part of a group in which it seemed that everyone emphasized being alike and doing things together—even dressing alike.

In order to charter a sorority on campus, there were many steps that had to be followed. First, there had to be an interest group. Knowing the need for having an African American sorority on campus, I decided to be a part of that group. At the time, it didn't matter to me what sorority would be chartered as long as we got one African American sorority on campus. In 1969, we were able to start our interest group. In 1970, the Alpha Kappa Alpha Sorority, a national sorority, was chartered on the campus of East Texas State University—the first of three to be chartered. I was again one of the firsts on East Texas State University's campus—a charter member of this sorority on campus. But as we had announced that we would be "pledging" this new sorority, and because the Pan Hellenic Council governed all sororities and fraternities on campus, we had to "pretend" that we were going through the whole cycle. This included "Rush." This meant that all young ladies had to attend "teas" or "receptions" at all of the sorority houses as if to see which sorority was interested in us and which sorority we wanted to be a part. As one might have expected, we were not invited back or invited to become a part of the "white" sororities. But our mission had been accomplished. We now knew the process and we were able to pledge Alpha Kappa Alpha Sorority, Inc. (At this time, the standards for Alpha Kappa Alpha were much higher than those of any of the other sororities.) We now would become active participants in the Pan Hellenic Council and an active sorority on campus.

During my years at East Texas State University, the number of "firsts" that I witnessed and often was a part of was innumerable. For example, once when I was sitting in the student center (probably waiting for Kenneth and Chief to get out of class, since we commuted daily), I was approached by two young men from the campus newspaper. They asked me if I would like to be featured in "The Brighter Side of ET." At the time, I don't think that I even knew what "The Brighter Side of ET" was. However, I soon learned that this was a feature in the campus news featuring campus beauties. Of course, I was honored to have my picture and a short write-up about me in the paper. This would be the first time that an African American had been featured. Later, I represented my sorority, Alpha Kappa Alpha, as a contestant in the Miss ET Pageant. I never really thought much of beauty pageants and could not imagine myself in one. However, I agreed and thus was one of two African American participants that year—a first for African Americans at the University.

Academically, the business department, which I had chosen as a major, did not seem to be a very warm department. This was not a racial problem; however, this was a communication problem. During the spring of 1970, I was fortunate enough to do my student teaching at Greenville Senior High School. In my opinion, at the time this was one of the largest and probably most progressive high schools in the area. Even though Greenville prided itself as being "The Blackest Land and the Whitest People," I felt that I fitted into the mostly white school environment quite well. However, during the 1970-71 school year, I became a work-study student in the Dean of Men's Office. It was through my work in this office that I decided that I wanted to receive my Master's Degree in this department, instead of the business department. I learned that the Guidance Department was a much more people-friendly department to be a part of—even for African Americans. So when I graduated in 1971, I had already begun my Master's Degree in Guidance.

I felt very proud for being a part of so many firsts at ETSU. However, the greatest reward was that I received two degrees from ETSU—my Bachelor's Degree in 1971 and my Master's Degree in 1973. Since commuting was not new, I commuted from Dallas to Commerce to obtain my Master's Degree.

My father had done graduate work at several universities, but he received his Master's Degree from ETSU. Unfortunately, when my father became principal at Sand Flat, the only way he could have gotten his Master's Degree would have been to move away from Emory. This would have been difficult because he was married and had a family (as well as a position that he cherished). My brothers—Jewel (Chief) and Harold—also received degrees from ETSU. At one time, my father, my brother (Chief) and I were all enrolled at the university at the same time.

Sports and Entertainment and ETSU

Attending East Texas State University opened other avenues for me. The university had sports teams, many clubs, held concerts, and brought many famous entertainers to the campus. For example, I can remember attending a concert where blues singer Lightning Hopkins performed in person. Another individual that I can remember is the writer, John Howard Griffin, the author of *Black Like Me*. Comedian Pat Paulson also appeared at a program while I was a student there. I also was fortunate enough to be able to take a course taught by folklorist J. Mason Brewer. At the time, I had no idea what this meant—he was one of the foremost folklorists in the area. But probably most impressive was the number of African American students that played football for the university that later went on to play professional football—and I knew them personally—Autry Beaman, Richard Houston, Jay Johnson, Chadwick Brown, Harvey Martin, and Dwight White, to name a few.

The Dallas ISD

Having been interviewed in the Placement Office on campus, I had hoped to be teaching in the Dallas Independent School District during the 1971-72 school year. However, after graduation, I moved to Dallas with my older brother, Alfred. At first, it was a visit, but I applied for a job through the Dallas Urban League the second week of my vacation. The next week I was working at Collins Radio as a secretary. Although I had gotten my degree and had hoped to be a teacher, I was so anxious to have a job that I gladly took the job at Collins Radio. Again, I was the first African American secretary in my department. I was well received by the other older, white females, but I soon discovered that I was not going to be happy working in such a controlled environment. I was using the skills that I wanted to teach others to use.

Two months after I started working at Collins Radio, I received a call at my brother's home after I had come home from work. It was Dr. Otto Fridia of the Dallas Independent School District. He asked if I would like to be a typing teacher at Hillcrest High School. I have always felt that I got this job for two reasons: (1) I was African American; and (2) I was at home. I feel that had I not answered the phone, he would probably have called the next name on his list. Again, I was about to become a part of another first. This time, it was the first time that Dallas had instituted a massive desegregation program. So I was a part of a group that would participate in many firsts. For me, I was teaching in the newly desegregated business department of Hillcrest High School.

Teaching at Hillcrest was probably more of an eye opener than attending Rains High School as one of the first African American students. By this time, I had attended an integrated high school, junior college, and university. I had done my student teaching at an integrated high school—although there were only a few African American students in my classes. But one thing I had missed in all of this exposure. I had never been familiar with the Jewish community. I knew nothing about the Jewish Religion and now I am assigned to Hillcrest High School. At the time I did not know it but it was sometimes referred to as "Hebrew High." In Emory, races generally meant black and white. In college, I had been a member of the International Club, so I was a friend to Africans and Asians. Somehow, I never knew much about the Jewish. I also must mention that they (Hillcrest students) were mostly wealthy too. While in Emory, I never knew much about wealth. In fact, I never knew anyone that was wealthy!

As a new teacher, I was eager to teach the children. I assumed that they would be accepting of me—and, in my opinion, they were. However, I think that it was probably the other white faculty members that lacked the sensitivity needed for this new venture. I feel that the transition here was very easy for me. I got along well with the African American teachers and the white teachers. However, because of the huge cultural and socio-economic differences between the students, the transition was not as easy for them. At Hillcrest, it was taking the poorest of the poor African American children and having them bused into the community of some of Dallas' most affluent individuals. This was not a good mix! There were constant problems that could have been avoided if the students on both sides of town could have been more sensitive to the type of school environment that they would be a part of and if all had known more about the backgrounds of the students involved.

I have been a part of the history making desegregation of my high school and college and then as a high school teacher in one of the state's largest school districts.

Pros and Cons of Desegregation

Growing up in Emory, Texas in the 1950's and 1960's in a segregated environment had a number of obvious disadvantages for African American youth. In many ways, Emory was the same as rural towns throughout Texas and throughout the United States. As an African American, I would never say that the advantages of segregation outweighed those of the desegregation of schools. But it is important to note that desegregation of the schools was an act that upgraded the educational level for African American children in a way that would never have occurred in the segregated school settings. Also, in America most families try to instill the "work ethic" into their children. Growing up in rural East Texas, young African

American students were never employed in the types of jobs that their counterparts in the white community took for granted as being jobs for students, i.e., the bank, grocery stores, restaurants, etc. However, desegregation often meant the closing of educational institutions that had been the centers of African American life and culture in these communities. Although many of the schools survived for a period, most of the African American schools were eventually closed and many were torn down because most had not been kept up to the standards of other schools. Because they were in the African American communities, they were not repaired or rehabilitated for continued use. Often, African American teachers and administrators were left without jobs or they were compelled to accept lesser jobs in order to remain employed. Fortunately, my father was not among those that were no longer employed in the same capacity. In 1965, when Rains High School was desegregated and students graduating from Sand Flat School were no longer bused to St. Paul High School in Greenville, my father's job remained as Principal of Sand Flat. However, when Sand Flat closed a few years later and the school district was completely integrated (desegregated), my father was hired as the principal of the middle school at Rains. Even though Sand Flat had closed, the former principal (my father) still lived in the community and still maintained the same relationship with his students that had attended Sand Flat.

Many students, parents, and teachers who had been a part of African American schools felt that even though academically there was much to be gained from having been able to be a part of the desegregation of the schools, there were also losses that resulted from this same process. For example, many African Americans believed that the overall education of the student suffered when it came to some of the character-building lessons that were a part of the African

American students' educational process when attending the segregated schools. Students probably had never heard such expressions as "Black Pride" or "Black Power." But in our own way, we had a sense of pride that gave us power to be the best that we could be; and that could not be equaled once we were no longer in our own environment. And for whatever reason, many students that had been very active in school and in extra-curricular activities often did not continue to be active in the same manner. Some students just did not believe that they "fit in." Consequently, they did not participate in the new environment.

Chapter 11
A Family Of My Own

When I was a teenager, I always imagined my being on my own, living in a beautiful apartment, and having a nice car. Since I thought that marriage and having a family were things that "just happened," I didn't really feel like I had to do a lot of planning for having a family. I just thought that "Mr. Right" would come along, we'd get married, and then the other things that are supposed to be a part of "the American Dream" (home, two children, a dog, and a picket fence) would all be added. This thought stayed with me throughout high school and throughout college. Most of my friends who had not gone to college had married, had children, etc. Some were even divorced. I really did not view this as a dream. Therefore, the American Dream was not my dream at all!

After being a single college graduate for a few years, I soon realized that "Mr. Right" only appeared after meeting numerous "Mr. Wrongs." I had experienced having my own apartment and having several nice cars. I realized that I was not as concerned as much about having the house, the husband, etc. as much as I was about having a child. I had enjoyed traveling, being able to shop, and enjoying most of the things that life had to offer a young, reasonably successful female. I decided that I needed someone with whom to share my life. As I said, I was single at the time so I decided that the best way that I could become a parent was to become an adoptive parent. I knew that having a little girl would fit into my lifestyle more than that of a little boy. Also, since adoption is not so much as what is best for you as it is what is best for the child, I thought that my lifestyle would fit into hers as well. Most of the things that I did socially, I could involve a little girl. Also, since I was living in an apartment, a little girl and I could share a smaller space with comfort.

When I talked over the possibility of adopting a child with my friends and family, the whole idea was met with mixed emotions. As far as my immediate family was concerned, they were very supportive from the onset. They knew that I was serious and they were willing to help in any way that they could. However, there were some (relatives and friends) that were skeptical. I received comments like "When you adopt a child, you don't know what you are getting." Of course, I answered with "When you have a child, you don't know what you are getting." I also explained to them that I was a teacher and of all of the problem children that I teach I could not recall that any of them were adopted. In other words, whether you know what you are getting or not, you can't predict everything. So once I decided that adoption was what I really wanted to do, I immediately started gathering information about starting the process. I got the application, which was the first step, and filled it out. Almost a year passed and it seemed that not much had been done. When I questioned why I had not heard anything yet, I was informed that the caseworker that was handling my file was no longer with the agency. This meant that my file was just sitting somewhere. So I started the process all over again. Within just a few months, the interviews and the home visits were held. My references had all checked out and I was approved for adoption. The next step was finding the child that I had said that I wanted—a young female, one that looked like she could be mine—African American.

Once I had decided that I was going to be a career woman (with a child), a funny thing happened. I met "Mr. Right." Before the adoption process was complete, I met the man who would become my husband—and my daughter's father—Theodore Maxwell Lawe. When the time came for me to meet my daughter—and eventually bring her home with me—it was agreed that I would get to know her first before introducing her to him. So for about two weeks, my time was devoted to getting to know my new daughter. Then, she and I went to dinner with Ted. This was their first meeting. Soon, I knew that this was a real family unit and we all began spending lots of time together—doing the things that families usually do. I adopted Sylvia as a single parent. I knew that I had made the right decision because the first thing that she said to me when we met was "Momma." I knew that this little girl was going to do her part in making this relationship work. After Ted and I were married, he adopted Sylvia also. Initially, Sylvia had referred to him as "Mr. Lawe." But soon after their meeting, it became "Daddy." The judge, who happened to be the same judge for both cases, told us that this was a rarity—the same child being adopted twice in such circumstances. I now had my own family. Soon after, we added the house and a cat. I guess this was my version of the American Dream!

Chapter 12
Living Life To The Fullest

When I was about five or six years old, I had unusually painful knee problems. For some reason, the pain always felt worse at night. Thanks to my mother and the rubbing alcohol I was able to endure this pain without really knowing why I was having the pain. All of my childhood, I can remember having this pain and resorting to the use of rubbing alcohol in order to get some relief. Actually, I think that my mother's hands were probably more soothing than the alcohol. It was difficult for me to explain the pain and probably even more difficult for my parents to understand that I had a serious problem.

In our house, we never focused on the negative things; instead, we focused on the positives. With this in mind, I just learned to live with pain and to accept my limitations. Among those limitations were walking for long distances and climbing stairs. This is not to say that I did not walk for long distances—I did. This does not mean that I did not climb stairs—I did. But I did these things with difficulty. Most children did not realize that these were difficult tasks for me. I did all of the things that the other children did. However, at night I suffered from having been involved in these activities.

As I grew into my teens, I noticed that most of the other young girls could do a few exercises that I could not do. I had problems touching my toes. At the time, I was a trim, seemingly healthy young lady; but I could not touch my toes. However, I was good at playing basketball, I was a good shot, and I had a good high kick when exercising in physical education classes. Therefore, touching my toes was not a real concern—I just knew that I could not. After all, young ladies don't bend to pick up things from the floor; they squat or kneel.

I first suspected that I had arthritis when I was about 16 or 17. My mother took me to the doctor (Dr. Lane) in Wills Point. At the time, this was probably the most popular doctor for African Americans in Emory. He did not give me a diagnosis of arthritis, but he gave me arthritis medicine. I thought that it was somewhat ironic that I was taking the same medication as one of my aunts (Aunt Gletha), who was taking it for arthritis also. I continued taking this medication on and off throughout college. Sometimes I would think that the illness was gone, and something would happen to let me know that it was still present. For example, once I was walking across the college campus while at East Texas State and it was raining. I had my umbrella up and I was well protected from the rain. However, as I was walking, suddenly my legs just completely failed to move. I could go no further! I stood there holding my umbrella for what seemed like minutes (even though it was probably only a few seconds) until my legs would continue moving. There were other similar instances when my legs just seemed to refuse to move. Occasionally, when climbing stairs, I would get at the top and could not go any further. Or, I would start down and could not continue to the bottom of the stairs. Fortunately, whenever this happened, it would only be for a short period. But for the most part, I always seemed quite healthy otherwise. Then, after not having problems for a while, I decided to stop taking the medication.

Upon moving to Dallas and becoming employed by the Dallas Independent School District, I had to have a physical examination. At the recommendation of a friend, I went to Dr. Mason, an African American doctor located on Forest Avenue in South Dallas (which is where most African American doctors where at that time). He was one of the most noted doctors in the community. I vividly remember going to Dr. Mason and having had a blood test. I was told that "sugar"(diabetes) showed up in the test. Since I had eaten before the test and had a soft drink with my lunch, he suggested that I come back on the following day before eating. I can remember that being a "very long" evening—wondering whether or not I was diabetic. As a lover of desserts, all I could think of was the banana pudding that I was planning to make (from scratch) that evening. I could not imagine being unable to eat all of the desserts and breads that I had always loved so much.

When I returned to Dr. Mason's office the next day for my blood test, much to my surprise and pleasure, I found out that what I had was "low" blood sugar. He said that it was just a little low and that it would just need to be monitored. Therefore, I had nothing to be worried about.

Since I had gone to Dr. Mason for my initial exam for working at the Dallas Independent School District, I decided that he would be my physician. I didn't know of any others anyway. For several years, when I had colds, flu, aches, pains, etc., I always went to Dr. Mason. It was Dr. Mason that finally told me that I did have arthritis. So, once again, I began taking arthritis medications. Once when I was ill, I went to another doctor because he was closer and I was driving myself. I had not taken the arthritis medication for a while. I was having stomach cramps and was very sick. He was concerned that I had stopped taking my medication. I told him that I had not been bothered with arthritis lately. He explained "there is no cure for arthritis and that I should continue taking the medication." He said that my not taking my medication had probably made me sick. I asked him "How long did I need to be on medication?" He said, "as long as you live." At this point, I could not believe that I would have to take any medication for the rest of my life—not for arthritis. I kept thinking "I'm young; I'm only in my twenties!" I decided that it was time that I started to read more about my illness and my medications.

A few years passed and I only had minor arthritis problems. One day while running a few errands, I decided to stop at a nearby Wyatt's Cafeteria in the Wynnewood Shopping Center. I can remember having minor difficulty walking inside. However, once inside, I could not walk any further. My legs seemed to have frozen. I could not move. This was very frightening. Somehow, with the assistance of my daughter, I was able to make it back to my car. It was at this point that I knew that I had to know what was going on with my body—my legs! At this time, Dr. Mason was no longer my physician. In fact, I think that the clinic where he had practiced was no longer there. Anyway, I had started going to a doctor (G.P.) at St. Paul Hospital by the name of Dr. Woodard. I called Dr. Woodard that afternoon and made an appointment for the next day. After many tests, Dr. Woodard explained to me that a very rare form of arthritis had shown up in my blood test. The rare disease was called Lupus. He said that I should not be too concerned and that he would order more tests. After taking more tests, I was pleased to hear that the Lupus did not show up. However, a short time after that, I was sick again and I was unable to walk. I thought it was the arthritis. I knew that arthritis affected all of my joints so I just took some time off from work hoping that my legs would get better and that I would not be ill anymore. Unfortunately, that did not happen. Not only were my legs hurting, I was very sick. Once again, I was back in Dr. Woodard's office trying to find out what was wrong with me. He ordered more tests. After getting the results of the tests, Dr. Woodward said that there was a specialist, Dr. Stanley Cohen, which he would like for me to see. However, Dr. Cohen was very expensive and I might not want to see him because of the cost. Although I respected Dr. Woodard, I was offended that he seemed to assume that I would not want to seek the help of a specialist because it was expensive. Even though my funds were somewhat scarce, I assured him that I would like the referral. I felt that he might have assumed that because I was African American, I could not afford Dr. Cohen.

When I entered Dr. Cohen's office, I was somewhat apprehensive. I had been upset with Dr. Woodard for telling me that he would be expensive, but now I was wondering just how expensive he would be. Just as when I had gone to the other doctors for arthritis problems, the first thing that is done is the drawing of the blood. However, this time it was different. Dr. Cohen came in and introduced himself. Except for the fact that he looked my age, I was very impressed. I had imagined that a specialist should be older. But for the first time, I had met a doctor that genuinely seemed to be interested in my illness and in me. This doctor sat down and described to me what Lupus is, who is usually affected by it (young African American women), and how I should be able to "live" with the illness. It was not very encouraging, however. I learned that prior to the 1950s, most women suffering with Lupus died in their 30s. At this point, I felt that maybe my future was not so bright! But with the knowledge that I gained from Dr. Cohen and from reading about the disease, I decided that I would just "live life to the fullest!" My disease would not keep me from doing the things that I enjoyed most. Therefore, I thought that one of the best ways to not be affected by having Lupus would be to not let anyone know that I have the disease—except a few people that are close to me. Before this writing, I have let this remain as "my illness" and I have not burdened others (even family and friends) with my complaints. This has often been very hard because of all of the illnesses that I have had that related back to my having Lupus. Also, I have had to take lots of medications and often the medications were (in my opinion) just as bad as being sick. In fact, sometimes I have taken medication to prevent the other medications from making me sick. I have even had to start going to an ophthalmologist on a regular basis because the Lupus medication can cause color blindness.

If having a disease that usually ends up in the death of the individual was not enough, you might say that I have also received what could be labeled as a second "death sentence." This all started with having a cough that I could not get to stop. For several years, I went to Dr. Cohen, as well as other primary care physicians (PCPs) in an effort to find out why I could not stop coughing. Because I have Lupus, it was thought that maybe it was connected to the disease. Therefore, I was sent to all kinds of specialists—ear, nose and throat specialists, lung specialists, etc. Also all kinds of tests (X-rays, swallowing tests, C T Scans of my lungs, sinuses, etc.) were given to determine the cause of the cough. However, no real conclusion was made. Therefore, the doctors just said that I had a respiratory problem, or infection.

For several years, I had complained that I thought that the air quality in my classroom was unsafe. I noticed that whenever school was in session, I always had problems coughing. Whenever school was not in session, my breathing was always better. Asbestos has been named as the cause of illness of a number of workers in the school district over the years. I even thought that perhaps the asbestos had affected me. But more than my being concerned about asbestos, I was concerned that the air that I was breathing in my classroom was not safe. At one time, the temperature in my classroom was averaging about 95 degrees and this was in January and February often when it was ice on the ground outside. I complained to the principal, the custodian, and basically anyone that would listen. Finally, I filed a grievance with the School District because I felt that this classroom was unsafe. Someone from Environmental Services came out, tested the air quality (and temperature). The ducts were cleaned and an air conditioning unit was placed in the classroom to be used during the winter months in order to circulate the air. This did help my breathing, but I cannot say that this was the solution. After a few more years of teaching in that classroom, and a number of more registered complaints, I was moved to the classroom across the hall. It is a bigger classroom, and the circulation is a little better. However, no one has ever given me copies of any of the tests that were performed to determine the air quality, as I had been promised. I just know that there were times that breathing was very hard.

From this point on, I had to be extremely careful whenever I had any kind of respiratory problem. And it was not long before I did have another incidence of sickness. This time, I was at home alone in the middle of winter. It was very cold and I was very sick. I considered calling an ambulance, but I decided that I was well enough to drive myself—big mistake! When I got to the doctor's office, I was too sick to sit up in the waiting room. After a short while, I was taken in to see the doctor (Dr. Waymon Drummond), at St. Paul Hospital. He in turn had the nurses get a wheel chair and he sent me on to the hospital to be admitted. After being admitted for pneumonia, and undergoing numerous tests, it was then that several specialists seemed to agree that my lungs had been extensively damaged. The first question that each would ask was "How long have you smoked?" They would not ask if I smoked—but how long? From this point on, Dr. Cohen seemed to have a better understanding of my illness and how to treat me for it. Until now, he had been my rheumatologist, but now he was my main doctor.

After having another serious bout of coughing, I went to the doctor and was given medication. Because I was really ill, the doctor gave me some samples and a prescription. When I got home, I took the medication and had the prescription filled. In less than an hour, I had to call 911 and was rushed to the hospital. Once again, I was admitted to St. Paul Hospital. This time Dr. Drummond warned me, that if I had not made it to the hospital when I did, I would probably have died. I was that near death! I had taken a medication that I was allergic to. It would seem that after all of the medications that I had taken, someone would have known of my allergy—even though I did not!

Once I survived the latest coughing bout and the reaction to the medication, I was recommended or referred to a pulmonary (lung) and asthma specialist, Dr. Pedro Zevallos. Dr. Zevallos began treating me for my lung disease. After frequent X-rays, CT scans, blood tests, etc., it was determined that my lungs were damaged (scarred) beyond repair. This was the first time that I had actually been told that there was no cure or no way of repairing my lungs. I was also told that this damage was not related to my having Lupus. Since the doctors have no way of determining when the scarring took place (or why), I would need to learn how to deal with two life-threatening diseases (Lupus and a lung disease). Therefore, I needed to be able to live with the disease and I needed to learn how to live life to the fullest! In other words, since there is no cure (just as there is no cure for Lupus), I needed to know how to live with the disease. One of the ways that he suggested that I start is that I take "therapy" (pulmonary and physical). He even suggested that at some point, I might be a candidate for a "lung transplant." Since I have already lived far beyond the normal life expectancy of an individual with Lupus and I have lived several years with a lung disease, I am convinced that I am handling my diseases and not letting them handle me! My plans are to just keep on defying the odds and—living life to the fullest!

Chapter 13
The "Farmer's Daughter" Arrives On Wolfwood

When I was born, my father had been in service and had come back and attended college—hardly a "farmer." But I guess because of the times, it would have been asking too much to place "college student" or "educator" as my father's profession on my birth certificate. It was not until I was a college graduate did I learn that this was on my birth certificate. At the time, I was quite alarmed. But as I grew older (and wiser) I realized what we are called or labeled is not important as long as we know who we are. That is why I feel that it is so important that we know our history and that our heirs carry on our legacy.

Because of my grandfather's being such a strong individual and imbedding the importance of family into my father's generation, I am proud to be able to carry on this family tradition.

Upon my graduating from ETSU, I moved to Dallas to live with my brother, Alfred, and his family. I had applied for several positions through the college placement center. However, I had not been hired by anyone upon graduation. So I got a job through the Dallas Urban

League to work at Collins Radio as a secretary, which is initially what I wanted to do. But it was when I applied for this job and had to obtain a copy of my birth certificate that I realized that it stated that my father's occupation was "farmer." Even though it did not matter what my father's occupation was at that time, I found it strange that he was listed on my birth certificate as a farmer. It took a while for me to get over this discovery!

After two weeks on this job at Collins, I was able to buy my first car—a new (1971) Oldsmobile Cutlass. This was possible because of my father, of course. I had always dreamed of my own apartment and a nice car. Soon after getting my car I also was able to move into my first apartment. For the first time in my life I was living my dream—on my own, my own apartment, and a nice car.

The job at Collins Radio only lasted for the summer. As I stated earlier, I got a call from Otto Fridia with the Dallas Independent School District. He asked if I'd like to teach at Hillcrest High School in Dallas. My answer—Yes! I taught at Hillcrest for five years.

Teaching at Hillcrest High School was a real learning experience for me. That was the first year of a massive desegregation and busing program in Dallas (1971). For the first time there were numerous African American faculty members and students at Hillcrest High School, as well as other previously all-white schools. This transition process was nothing like what I had experienced at Rains. This was in part because of the socio-economic differences of the students involved. Hillcrest had some of Dallas' richest and poorest students. The best part of this whole situation is that I truly felt that I was needed. And I think that the students felt that way too.

After five years at Hillcrest, I was transferred to Thomas Jefferson High School—only minutes away from Hillcrest. However, Thomas Jefferson was more racially and socio-economically balanced. In

1976 when I first began teaching at Thomas Jefferson High School the ethnic breakdown was almost equal (one-third white, one-third Mexican, and one-third African American). This racial diversity soon changed to a large percent of the student body's being Hispanic and only a few African Americans and even fewer whites.

Thanks to my father, Mrs. Washington, and Mrs. Shiflet, I feel that I have been very successful as a teacher. Thanks to my parents I have been successful as a productive citizen, a good parent, and a loving wife. But I will always be appreciative for the wonderful upbringing in Emory and for all of those who had a hand, i.e., aunts, uncles, teachers, my pastor (Reverend Cleveland Alexander), and Sunday school teachers (Mrs. Furiel Johnson and Mrs. Alene Randolph).

During my youth, I never imagined that I would have been a teacher for most of my life. I knew that my father had been a teacher and that I had numerous cousins that were teachers. What I did not know was that both my father's grandparents (McMillan) were teachers. So I guess that I just followed a tradition—without knowing it. And who really cares if my birth certificate says that I am the daughter of a farmer? I know that I came from a long line of educators.

Chapter 14
The A.C. McMillan African American Museum

The A. C. McMillan African American Museum is an institution for organizing relevant materials of the African American community within a historical and cultural context. Museums are vehicles that have broad community support and perpetual existence. The McMillan Museum is no exception. The Museum's development is an indicator of growth on the part of African Americans living in Emory, Texas. It is dedicated to the memory of my father, A. C. McMillan, for his contributions to the education and development of African Americans and other youth in Rains County. At the Museum, the history of the McMillans and the history of African Americans in Rains County may continue to be documented as I write this history and in the years to come.

The general objectives of the A. C. McMillan African American Museum are:

- To serve as a depository for historical and significant

events affecting African Americans in the Rains County
area;

- To serve as a neutral point and bridge between racial and
  ethnic groups;
- To instill a sense of identity and pride in African American
  students; and
- To serve as a leadership development institution for
  the African American community in and around Rains
  County.

After the official opening, serious attention has been given to
developing a relationship with the Rains County Genealogical Society,
The Rains County Historical Society, The East Texas Historical
Association, The East Texas Genealogical Association, The National
Trust for Historic Preservation, Texas Historical Commission and the
National Commissions for the Arts and Humanities, and the Rains
County Library.

Some of the exhibits that have received many visitors and media
coverage are: The Buffalo Soldiers Exhibit, The Negro Baseball Leagues
Exhibit, Reconstruction in Texas, and African Americans Featured
on Commemorative Postage Stamps, , The Dolls of Color Exhibit,
The Civil Rights Movement—Brown vs. Board of Education Exhibit,
and The Rosenwald Schools in the South, Pioneer African American
Families in Rains County, and Jim Crow Racial Stereotypes.

Through the A.C. McMillan African American Museum, the
history of the McMillans of Rains County will continue to be
documented. Thus, African Americans and non-African Americans
will have a venue for studying the accomplishments and the history
of African Americans in Rains County in particular, and the United
States as a whole.

Chapter 15
McMillans In The 2000'S

Since the opening of the A. C. McMillan African American Museum in February 2000, my whole outlook on family history and African American heritage has taken on new meaning. As I mentioned earlier, the opening of the museum had a big change in my mother's life, also. After being free to volunteer for several different civic organizations, she now has what basically is a full-time commitment. However, I do feel that this is a positive. She has acted as the museum's only staff person that is at the museum during all of its opening hours. (She has logged hundreds of hours at the Museum.)

When the museum opened, there were approximately seven ladies that signed on as the volunteer staff. Assisting my mother on a regular basis were: Mrs. Audie Shiflet (my former business teacher), Mrs. Esta Mae Peeples (a former teacher who taught at Rains also), and Mrs. Adine Thomas (who worked at Rains for many years). Others were my aunts: Mildred Garrett, Florene McMillan, Modean Lane, and Claressa McMillan. Two of my uncles—Fannon and Dave Garrett—also were volunteers and supporters of the Museum's many events. However, over a period of time, whether because of death, health reasons or job restrictions, that number has decreased. However, most are still physically able to spend some time at the museum.

My Continued Search of McMillan History

The opening of the A. C. McMillan African American Museum has opened many avenues for my study of genealogy in the African American community in Emory and in the McMillan family in particular. The museum has brought such visitors as the Lemmon McMillan family (now residing in Illinois and California) whom I mentioned earlier. Also, because of their visit, my Uncle P.W. McMillan made his first (and only) visit to the Museum that I can recall. Several reunions (which are held annually) also have enabled relatives from out-of-town to visit the Museum. Although the Museum is now in its tenth year (2010), there are still relatives in Rains and other neighboring counties that have not paid their first visit. However, this is not discouraging. We would rather like to emphasize the number of normally non-museum goers that frequent the museum. In fact, that is the category for most of our visitors. For many, the A. C. McMillan African American Museum is the first (and only) museum that they have ever visited. Therefore, we feel an obligation to those individuals to present a very positive image.

I guess that one of the highlights of my life in the year 2002 was being named one of 10 women throughout the United States to receive the Quaker Oats and the National Council of Negro Women's "Woman of Wonder Award." My daughter, Sylvia, nominated me for this award, but I am not sure how I was chosen. In 2003, I was nominated for and received a fellowship to study at the Smithsonian Institution as a Visiting Professional in the Smithsonian Affiliations Program. This meant moving to Washington, D.C. for a month during the summer. At my age, this was really a different kind of experience for me, but it was one of the most rewarding experiences I have had in my professional life.

In 2004 and 2005, I received a Diversity Scholarship to attend the National Trust for Historic Preservation in Louisville, Kentucky and Portland, Oregon respectively. Fortunately, in 2010, I received a Texas Scholars scholarship to attend this same conference in Austin, Texas. I received these scholarships to further my study of the Rosenwald Schools and their significance in the South and in Rains County specifically. Also, in 2005, with the assistance of several loyal Richland School and Sand Flat School alumni, the museum sponsored an all-school reunion that was held in conjunction with the museum's fifth anniversary. It was also a part of the Emory Founders Day activities. It was our hope that funds raised from these reunions would assist in our being able to restore the Sand Flat School building for future use and to obtain historic markers for the Sand Flat and the Richland School sites. Unfortunately, we have not been able to raise the necessary funds for reaching our goals.

Since the opening of the museum in 2000, I have become affiliated with several organizations that I probably would not have ever considered—the Rains County Genealogical Society, the East Texas Historical Association (where my husband Ted is on the Board and is the immediate past President of the Association) and I am on the Membership Committee), the Texas Association of Museums, and the African American Association of Museums. Rains County historian Elaine Bay and Connie Dollins, President of the Genealogical Society, have both been very helpful in my gaining information about the McMillans and Rains County. Also, the *Rains County Leader* has been very helpful. There are numerous articles in previous issues that give lots of information that I would not have gotten otherwise.

Being the Director of the Museum has also resulted in my being called upon to do speaking engagements and to accompany my husband, Ted, as he is called upon to speak to many of the associations of which we are both involved. (He is the "real" historian.) This enables both of us to not only find ways of studying East Texas history, but it also serves as an avenue to put The A. C. McMillan African American Museum in a positive light in East Texas and throughout the state.

One of the most important ways of gathering family history is from the human resources that are available. That is why it is important to take advantage of the wealth of knowledge those relatives such as my mother (Modis McMillan), Aunt Modean (Lane), Aunt Florene (McMillan), Uncles Fannon and Dave (Garrett), Aunt Mildred (Garrett) and Aunt Claressa (McMillan) have offered. I received some information from Richard (Dwight) Tolliver, the son of Dorothy Tolliver and the grandson of Ora Murray (my grandfather's sister). I have also been able to get information from other relatives such Doris (Faye) Taylor, the daughter of Otto Malone and the granddaughter of Olma Malone (my grandfather's sister).

Finally, the Internet is by far the most helpful way of gathering information of individuals that perhaps would not sit down and actually give an historian an interview, but will take the time to respond to e-mails. I have also made use of genealogy websites, as well as surname searches.

During the summer of 2004, I decided that I should get back to work on writing my family history and try to at least get it to a point that I would feel comfortable going to the printer with it. So, I began going to the Dallas Public Library on a regular basis. I had been communicating with a woman that had been referred to me by Elaine Bay. This woman, Patty Macsisak, had been doing research on her husband's family, the Woosleys. She said that she felt that there was a connection between the "white" Woosleys and the "black" Woosleys. She shared her notes with me on the Woosleys, and to both of our surprise, many of the individuals that she had researched were indeed "black" but were labeled as "white" on the U.S. Census Records. Because many of these individuals were my relatives and I had known them, I was able to identify many of those that she had as white in her records. Our going to the library was really an inspiration for me. For the rest of the summer, I often went to the library and worked all day. Often I worked on programs that had databases that I did not have at home. However, some days I went to the library just because I could dedicate the whole day working on my project. My grandson, Preston, also went to the library with me on numerous occasions. When he is older, I feel that he will have a much better appreciation of reading his family's history when he recalls all those days that we spent at the Dallas Public Library. In fact, he will probably feel that he was instrumental in writing his family's history!

Once I began working at the Public Library and researching U.S. Census Records, it confirmed my belief that I could not write a history of the McMillan family without including most of the families of the Emory communities of Sand Flat, Wolf, and Jacksonville. Therefore, I decided to include most of the families from the Sand Flat, Wolf, and Jacksonville communities. After all, we are all connected. With the use of the U.S. Census Records, I was able to connect to relatives that I knew were my relatives, but I did not know the connection. Through the use of these databases, I have now discovered much more than I ever intended when I started out to write the history of the McMillans of Emory, Texas. As I mentioned earlier, I am not a "historian." However, I have become an avid admirer of family history. Through my association with several organizations and my involvement in The A. C. McMillan African American Museum, many avenues have been made available for me to pursue my interests in writing my family's history.

Chapter 16
Living On Wolfwood

As a child in Emory, Texas, I never could have imagined the life that I am living on "Wolfwood Lane." When I moved to Dallas, Texas in 1971, I had dreams of being on my own in the big city; but never in my wildest dreams did I think that I could have enjoyed all of the pleasures that life has had to offer.

For a short while, I lived with my older brother, Alfred, when I first moved to Dallas. Later I moved into my own apartment (which would be the first of approximately six apartments). I truly liked apartment living. One reason I liked living in apartments was that you only had to take care of your living quarters. I consider myself an indoor person, so I really did not care whether I had a yard or not. As a young single, my friends Hella and Lois and I often spent our Sunday evenings looking at apartments and later we started looking at houses. It was a good pastime for Sundays and it seemed that one of us was always in the market for a new apartment. Finally, I decided to begin looking at houses. After becoming a mother and growing a little older, I decided that perhaps home ownership should be the next step. After all, I felt that Sylvia, my daughter, should be able to live in a house and have a yard. Although I had always lived in Dallas since moving away after college, I found my first new home in Mesquite. It was what many called "a starter" home. However, we lived there for approximately 20 years. That is where I was living when I got married and stayed there until in 2000 when we decided to move back into Dallas.

Ted has always had several professions; and in 2000 he was a real estate investor. The housing market in Dallas was doing extremely well and many individuals (Ted as well) made lots of money buying and selling houses. We decided that it was also a good time for us to begin looking for a new home. We were looking in various areas of the Dallas Metroplex. After all, at this time we would not have to be concerned with what school district our daughter would be attending. Often, Ted and I would ride to the various houses that were being remodeled or repaired for resale. Generally, the houses were not houses that I was interested in owning, even though we were looking for a house for ourselves. However, Ted had purchased a house and he constantly made references to the house—its size, its yard, its location, etc. Then one day, he told me that ironically the woman next door was from Rains County—Ginger—a community outside of Emory. When I went to look at the house, I met the neighbor. Her name was Arrie Lou Duncan. Little did I know that I would eventually move into the home that was initially going to be put up for sale and that "Lou" would become one of my dearest friends. Well, that is exactly what happened. When Ted and his crew were near completion of the remodeling and repairs, we decided that we liked the home for ourselves.

Because I was teaching and because I was still quite comfortable with the house in Mesquite, I did not feel an urgency to move into our new home. Ted started moving a little at a time and for a while we were actually living in two places. Finally, he got the movers to pack things away and move them to our new home on Wolfwood.

Of all of the years that we lived in Mesquite, I lived in a nice neighborhood with good neighbors. However, it was not until I moved to Wolfwood Lane that I really knew what having true neighbors meant. I found that "true neighbor" in Lou. It was very much like when I lived in Emory ("Wolf"). She was that kind of neighbor. I guess one of the most interesting things about our relationship, although we are both from Rains County, at the time that she lived there (even if I had been born then) we probably would have never known each other. That was at a time when everything was segregated so our paths probably would not have ever crossed. I'm sure that she never dreamed of having a good friend that was African American just as she never dreamed of having an African American next door. How lucky we both are that we met at the time that we did. She is an excellent cook and a great seamstress. Ted and I benefit from both. She often tailors my clothing and cooks for us too. She bakes some of the best desserts imaginable—some from recipe books and some are her own creations. My favorite is her Earthquake Cake. I've never had one like it anywhere else. Lou is also a "shop-a-holic." So, quite naturally, we go shopping together. We also eat at each other's houses as well as go out to eat together. And, since I am talking about neighbors, on Wolfwood I have other neighbors that I must mention. Lou lives on the left and Norma and Charles are my neighbors on the right. Amy lives across the street with her two sons. Then there is Shirley Dry, who is also a good friend of Lou's (and now a good friend of mine). Lou, Shirley, Norma, and I have had brunch, lunch, and even a tea together. Lou is the one that does most of the cooking, so Shirley (who is a retired teacher) and I often have coffee, snacks, etc. at Lou's.

Lou has an expression "You cannot say no to Lou." However, when it comes to eating her good cooking—who would want to say no?

Since living on Wolfwood, Ted has continuously made changes and improvements to the landscape of the property. Probably one of the most loved improvements is that he had the patio and a picnic area in our backyard stoned, added lighting, and lawn furniture for entertaining outside. Although I am not an outdoor person, I must admit that he has made it appealing to me also. At least about once a year Ted prepares dinner for several of our friends—usually my former church members from Memorial—Alversia Vinson, (Sister) Maple McGhee, Leola Black, and Diane Cline, and close friends Hella Mayberry, Donnie Landy, Florence (Faye) Cox, and Lois Lane. Of course, neighbors Lou and Shirley are always invited and so is my friend from work, Barbara Roth. Grandsons Preston and Blair also enjoy this same area in the summertime because it is this area where their aboveground pool is during the summer months.

In recent years, things are really changing in our city as well as our neighborhood. However, Ted and I are really blessed to have moved into this neighborhood and to have had the opportunity to know our neighbors. Life is good on Wolfwood Lane!

Conclusion

It was not until after the death of my father, A. C. McMillan, that I started gathering family history. Fortunately, I have handwritten notes that my father had that recorded many family births, deaths, marriages, etc. After seeing these notes, I started gathering other family history and family photographs. This effort has not been as successful as I had hoped. Therefore, at the time of the printing of this history, it will not be as up to date as I had planned. However, I do want to give credit to some relatives that I have recently met because of my constant use of the Internet and the telephone. I have been communicating by telephone with Lottie McMillan, my father's first cousin who lives in Denver, Colorado. Another distant cousin, Karla Ross, who lives in Memphis, Tennessee, has contacted me by email. We have communicated several times and she specifically had information regarding Dr. Julius A. McMillan who was a surgeon and on the faculty of Meharry for 45 years. He spent summers at the Mayo Clinic and two summers at the Crile Clinic. Dr. McMillan held the medical director's post at the George W. Hubbard Hospital continuously from 1925 to 1927. Also, for the past two years, another cousin—Avis Dean Lewis—has attended the McMillan Reunion and she has given me information on the Deans, descendants of Perla

McMillan Dean, sister of my grandfather—Jewel H. McMillan. This information will be added to the "Pioneer African American Families of Rains County" at the A.C. McMillan African American Museum.

When I was in elementary school and in high school, I never took any courses in African American History. I don't think that I even heard of African American History or Black History until I was about to graduate from college. Even though I never took such courses, my education in African American history has come from outside the classroom. My first book report in elementary school was on the book entitled, *Up from Slavery*, by Booker T. Washington. When I read the same book a few years ago, I can't say that I remembered very much of it from that first reading. Because such books were never required reading when I was growing up, had it not been for my father's interest in my being aware of African American History, I would have had an even more limited knowledge of African American History. Even then, my father subscribed to such magazines as *Ebony* and *Jet* and such newspapers as the *Post Tribune* and *The Kansas City Call.*

Knowing how the African Americans were an important part of the history of this nation and how they were totally left out of the history books, I understand the importance of history's being accurately written. In doing my family's genealogy, I have discovered that my ancestors, as well as other African Americans in Rains County, valued an education and played an important role in the education of African Americans in Rains County beginning in the 1800s and continued until the 1980s—the time of my father's retirement from the Rains Independent School District. In order to be sure that our history is accurately written, we must write it ourselves, or at least be a part of the process. There is an African saying, "Until the lion has its own historian, the hunter will always be glorified." Likewise, because I am the writer of this history, there is more about my family and me—for obvious reasons.

Appendix A
1897 County Treasurer's School Account Register[6]

I have been told that my great-grandparents, Alfred and Dora McMillan were the first African American teachers in Rains County. Though I have not found any records to document that, I have not found any to say that they were not either. In the <u>1897 County Treasurer's School Account Register,</u> it lists payments to Dora McMillan for "teaching" in 1896, 1897, and 1898. During that same time period, payments were made to A.D. Session, W. C. M. Manly, A.S. Session, and Henery Guiden. A.S. Session is listed for teaching in Richland #9; Dora McMillan is listed for teaching in Emory (col) #1 and Isiah Bunkley (col) #19; and Henry Guiden is listed for teaching in Emory (col) #1. Dora McMillan is listed in the U.S. Census Records as a Mulatto. There are stories of her husband, Alfred McMillan, being arrested for being married to a "white" woman. In all of the records pertaining to teachers during this period, I do not find any payments made to Alfred McMillan. This question comes to mind because he is

6 <u>1897 County Treasurer's School Account Register,</u> <u>www.rootsweb.com/~txrains/County</u> School Report.

listed as "Black" in the U.S. Census Records. At this time, there were four "Colored" schools listed in Rains County: Emory #1, Chapel Hill #5, Richland #9, and Isiah Bunkley #19.

Appendix B:
Teaching Certificates, Early 1900s[7]

Since I am a teacher, and I now know that I came from a line of teachers, e.g., my father (A. C. McMillan), my great-grandfather (Alfred "A. C." McMillan), and my great-grandmother (Dora McMillan), I am more interested in knowing the teachers in the African American community before me. Before my research, I did not realize that I was a part of such an important legacy in the history of Rains County. I am honored to be a part of this history in Rains County—that of the early African American educators. This shows that those pioneers in education had a desire to teach, even though their circumstances seemed dire.

Teaching certificates issued in and for Rains County were listed in the County Judge's office. The County Judge once served as the County Superintendent of schools. A person employed in Rains County had to register his/her certificate with the County Judge/Superintendent. The date of the registration of the certificate indicates when an individual taught in Rains County. Most certificates expired either two or four

---

7 www.txgenes.com/txrains/teachers.htm.

years from the date of issuance. Listed below are some of the African American teachers who taught in Rains County in the early 1900's.

Albritton, Bessie H. – colored/female, Greenville, Nativity: Texas, date issued: 04/20/1927, date of registration: 08/04/1927.

Alexander, Tommie. – colored/female, Point, Nativity: Texas, date issued: 08/16/1924, date of registration: 10/27/1924.

Anderson, Emmett, colored/male, Marshall, Texas, Nativity: Texas, date issued: 05/15/1920, date of registration: 07/12/1927.

Anderson, Mrs. F.A., colored/female, Route, 2, Point, Nativity: Texas, date issued: 08/08/1932, date of registration: 05/27/1933.

Baker, J.P., colored/male, Ft. Worth, Nativity: Texas, date issued: 06/05/1900, date of registration: 08/27/1915, expired: permanent.

Bennett, Cora, colored/female, Marshall, Texas, Nativity: Texas, date issued: 08/07/1924, date of registration: 10/01/1925.

Bowers, Jackie, colored/female, Clarksville, Nativity: Texas, date issued: 05/21/1923, date of registration: 10/31/1925.

Brown, Lillie Bille, colored/female, Point, Nativity: Texas, date issued: 09/03/1928, date of registration: 10/17/1928.

Caiss, Florence, colored/female, Point, Nativity: Texas, date issued: 09/06/1915, date of registration: 09/06/1915.

Choyce, Martha, colored/female, Tyler, date of registration: "extended 1 year

Date of registration, 12/18/1928. Age: 29.

Coger, Mary C., colored/female, Emory, date issued: 04/12/1934, date of registration: 10/16/1931.

Coger, (Dunkin), Mary Elizabeth, colored/female, Emory, Nativity: Texas, date issued: 09/91/1931, date of registration: 10/09/1933, Age: 40, years experience in Texas: 6.

Cooper, Ennis C., colored/male, Point, Nativity: Texas, date issued: 07/31/1913, date of registration: 04/03/1915.

Crayton, Narva Nay Lewis, colored/female, Point, Nativity: Texas, date issued: 09/01/1942, date of registration: 07/17/1945, age: 25, years experience in Texas: 5, years experience in other states: 0.

Cullors, J.W., colored/male (Professor Cullors was one of Sand Flat's first teachers. He came shortly after my great-grandmother, Dora McMillan, who was teaching until at least 1898, according to courthouse records, and died in 1907), Emory, Nativity: Texas, date issued: --/01/1912, date or registration 06/30/1915.

Cullors, Mrs. Lula, colored/female, Emory, Nativity: Texas, date issued: 08/18/1923, date of registration: 09/19/1923, Age: 32, years experience in Texas: 25.

Cyphers, Nolia, colored/female, San Antonio, date issued: 05/31/1926, date of registration: 11/06/1926.

Daniel, Maudie, colored/female, Point, Nativity: Texas, date issued: 08/16/1919, date of registration: 10/12/1920, age: 22, years experience in Texas: 3.

Edwards, Mrs. Deborah, colored/female, Longview, Box 615, Nativity: Texas, date issued: 02/04/1921, date of registration: 10/25/1921, age: 20, years experience in Texas: 1.

Edwards, Miss Frankie Lou, colored/female, Nativity: Texas, date issued: 09/01/1942, date of registration: 09/09/1944, years experience in Texas: 0, years of experience in other states: 0.

Edwards, Omae L., (later became Mrs. Omae Wesley, wife of Prof. C. C. Wesley) colored/female, Point, Nativity: Texas, date issued: 08/24/1931, date of registration: 09/12/1931, age: 21, years experience in Texas: 3,
Date issued: 09/01/1937, date of registration: 09/13/1937, age: 27, years experience in Texas: 8.

Edwards, Ona Lillian, colored/female, Point, Nativity: Texas, date issued: 06/06/1929, date or registration: 08/08/1929, age: 18, date issued 07/02/1935, date of registration: 07/19/1935, age: 25, years experience in Texas: 7.

Fudgens, Nannie, colored/female, Lone Oak, Nativity: Texas, date issued: 11/06/1920, date of registration: 12/17/1920.

Gilmore, Olivia, colored/female, (later became Mrs. Olivia Scales, who died recently at over 100 years of age), Wolf City, date issued: 04/07/1927, date of registration: 11/03/1928, age: 26, years experience in Texas: 6.

Graves, Johnnie Lee, colored/female, Marshall, Nativity: Texas, date issued: 05/24/1927, date of registration: 09/18/1928, age: 22, years experience in Texas: 1.

Hall, Mrs. Beulah E., colored/female, Dallas, Nativity: Texas, date issued: 09/03/1920, date of registration: 09/18/1928, age: 22, years experience in Texas: 4.

Hall, Pauline Mary, colored/female, Big Sandy, Texas, Nativity: Texas, date issued: 09/01/1945, date of registration: 01/28/1946, age: 25, years experience in Texas: 3, years experience in other states: 0.

Hobdy, Miss Lucy Mae, colored/female, date issued: 09/01/1939, date of registration: 11/22/1943, years experience in Texas: 3, years experience in other states: 0.

Holman, Zephy, colored/female, Point, Nativity: Texas, date issued: 06/03/1922, date of registration: 10/30/1923, age: 29, years experience in Texas: 10.

Irwing, Ernest A., colored/male, Box 237, Marshall, Nativity: Texas, date issued: 0511/1908 (permanent), date of registration: 10/25/1921.

Iwing, (possibly "Irwing") Mrs. W. B., colored/female, Marshall, Nativity: Texas, date issued: 09/01/1920 (permanent), date of registration: 10/07/1922, age: 34, years experience in Texas: 9.

Jackson, Cecilia, colored/female (related to my mother), Emory, Nativity: Texas, date issued: 09/10/1920, date of registration: 09/20/1920, age: 19, years experience in Texas: 0.

Johnson, Charles King, colored/male, Nativity: USA, date issued: 09/01/1939, date of registration: 07/14/1943, age: 32, years experience in Texas: 5.

Johnson, Miss Gertrude Ione (Wilson), colored/female, Nativity: USA, date issued: 09/01.1938, date of registration: 07/14/1943, age: 28, years experience in Texas: 10.

King, Harvey F., colored/male, Emory, date issued: 05/17/1921, date of registration: 10/07/1930, age: 47, years experience in Texas: 22.

Lamkin, Hodge, colored/female, Emory, Nativity: Texas, date issued: 08/09/1927, date of registration: 09/--/1927, age: 25, years experience in Texas: 15.

Lanken, W.M., colored/male, *Marshall, Texas, Nativity: Texas, date issued: 06/06/1927, age: 54, years experience in Texas: 30.*

Lee, Will Douglas, colored/male, R.F.D. 5, Sulphur Springs, Texas, Nativity: American, date issued: 08/25/1928, date of registration: 05/08/1941, age: 40, years experience in Texas: 6.

Leggett, Mrs. Ethel, colored/female, Point, Nativity: Texas, date issued: 09/08/1934, date of registration: 09/18/1934, age: 39, years experience in Texas: 10, date issued: 09/01/1936, date of registration: 09/18/1936, age: 42, years experience in Texas: 11, years experience in other states: 0, date issued: 08/31/1937, date of registration: 09/14/1937, age: 42, years experience in Texas 12, years experience in other states: 0.

Lewis, Robert A.W., colored/male, Point, Nativity: Texas, date issued: 09/01/1941, date of registration: 07:17/1945, age: 28, years experience in Texas: 4, years experience in other states: 0.

Mallard, Lexie Etta Price, colored/female, (Mrs. Lexie Mallard taught my parents at Sand Flat, and she taught me at St. Paul High School.) Emory, Nativity: Texas, date issued: 09/01/1936, date of registration: 09/28/1936, age: 32, years experience in Texas: 13, years experience in other states: 0, date issued: 08/16/1937, date of registration: 08/26/1937, age: 33, years experience in Texas: 14.

Manley, Caulie Margie, colored/female, Nativity: Texas, date issued: 08/24/1925, date of registration: 07/24/1926, age: 23, years experience in Texas 2, date issued: 09/01/1933, date of registration: 06/28/1947, age: 36, years experience in Texas: 10, years experience in other states: 1.

Manley, William C.M., colored/male, Emory, date issued: 08/31/1925, date of registration: 03/11/1927, age: 56, years experience in Texas: 28.

Manley, Delphine Myrtis, colored/female, Temple, Texas, Nativity: Texas, date issued: 08/08/1935, date of registration 10/12/1935, age: 23, years experience in Texas: 0, years experience in other states: 0.

Mitchell, Mrs. Lucie, colored/female, date issued: 05/15/1920, date of registration: 10/07/1930, age: 30, years experience in Texas: 10.

Moore, Esther V., colored/female, (Mrs. Esther Moore was the mother of Florene McMillan, the wife of my uncle Elbert McMillan.), Marshall, Nativity: Texas, date issued: 08/27/1922, date of registration: 06/23/1932, age: 31, years experience in Texas: 10.

Murdock, Mrs. Lendora, colored/female, Nativity: "Negro," date issued: 04/26/1940, date of registration: 09/18/1943, age: 34, years experience in Texas: 10.

Murdock, Nathaniel H., colored/male, Point, **Nativity**: Texas, date issued: 08/16/1933, date of registration: 08/10/1934, age: 25, years experience in Texas: 2, date issued: 08/31/1937, date of registration: 09/29/1937, age: 29, years experience in Texas: 5.

Porter, Pansy Lucile, colored/female, Point, Texas, Nativity: Texas, date issued: 09/01/1933, date of registration: 10/21/1933, age: 29, years experience in Texas: 7.

Pratt, Emma, colored/female, Greenville, Nativity: Texas, date issued: 09/04/1920, date of registration: 10/22/1920.

Pruitt, J.W., colored/male (married to Jennie Pruitt, sister of my aunt, Nina Robinson), Creek, Texas, Nativity: Texas, date issued: 08/28/1931, date of registration: 10/19/1931, age: 27, years experience in Texas: 6.

Reece, Cleo, colored/female, Emory, Nativity: Texas, date issued: 08/12/1934, date of registration: 12/20/1934, age: 23, years experience in Texas: 5.

Reeder, Malissia G., colored/female (married Junion Murray, my mother's cousin), Emory, Texas, Nativity: Texas, date issued: 10/01/1945, date of registration: 10/05/1945, age: 35, years experience in Texas: 3, date issued: 05/16/1946, date of registration: 07/02/1946, residence: Hawkins, Texas, age: 36, years experience in Texas: 4.

Russell, Mrs. J. V., colored/female, Point, Nativity: Texas, date issued: 08/06/1923, date of registration: 10/25/1926, years experience in Texas: 0, years experience in other states: 0.

Sanders, Mable, colored/female, Point, Nativity: Texas, date issued: 06/16/1919 (permanent), date of registration: 10/30/1923, age: 29, years experience in Texas: 10.

Scales, Ms. Olmir, colored/female, Wash----, date issued: 10/15/1929, date of registration: 11/02/1929, age: 27, years experience in Texas: 2.

Stevenson, Odelle Ivy, colored/female (Mrs. Stevenson is my

mother's cousin. She resides in Los Angeles, California.), Emory, Nativity: American, date issued: 08/31/1939, date of registration: 09/16/1940, age: 24, years experience in Texas: 0.

Swanson, Vivian Edna, colored/female, Marshall, Nativity: Texas, date issued: 05/31/1927, date of registration: 09/29/1927, age: 19.

Thornton, D.H., colored/male, Marshall, date issued: 10/11/1925, date of registration: 12/01/1925, age: 32, years experience in Texas: 5, years experience in other states: 1.

Turner, Curlie Jenkins, colored/female, Point, Texas, date issued: 08/31/1942, date of registration: 01/25/1941.

Underwood, (Deggett), Luvera, colored/female, Point, Nativity: Texas, date issued: 08/16/1926, date of registration: 12/10/1927, age: 22, years experience in Texas: 2.

Watkins, Eddie Renn, colored/male, Point, Nativity: Texas, date issued: 07/03/1934, age: 30, years experience in Texas: 5.

Watson, Miss Wilma, colored/female, Emory, Texas, Nativity: Texas, date issued: 06//01/1943, date of registration: 09/30/1944, age: 22, years experience in Texas: 0, years experience in other states: 1.

Wesley, Cyreonion Climie, colored/male (He was known as Professor C. C. Wesley during my lifetime. He was the Principal at Richland School, when my father was Principal at Sand Flat.), Point, Nativity: Texas, date issued: 09/1939, date of registration: 06/13/1942, age: 38, years experience in Texas: 4.

Wright, Katherine Gladys, colored/female, date issued: 08/11/1930, date of registration: 04/18/1941, age: 28, years experience in Texas: 8.

Wright, Snodie M., colored, date issued: 08/16/1926, date of registration: 10/09/1930.

Appendix C
Some Of The Recorded
Deaths In The Early McMillan Family
In The 1800'S And Early 1900'S*

- Emma Flourney died November 28, 1881. (I do not know the relationship.)
- Mary Jane McMillan (Alfred's mother) died March 6, 1882. This was my great-great grandmother.
- Clide Dean died August 28, 1900. This was Perla's son.
- Dora McMillan, my great-grandmother, died February 27, 1907.
- Alfred Otis McMillan (son of John and Montegg McMillan) died December 5, 1907. (Alfred Otis McMillan was born May 18, 1907.)

This information was recorded in the notes of my father, A. C. McMillan. He had copied this information from Aunt Olma's Bible (sister of Jewel McMillan, my grandfather).

ABOUT THE AUTHOR

Gwendolyn McMillan Lawe was born in Emory, Texas, (in the "Wolf Community") the only daughter of A.C. and Modis McMillan. She attended Sand Flat School (in Emory, Texas), St. Paul High School (in Hunt County), and graduated from Rains High School (in Emory). Among the first of Sand Flat (an African American only elementary school) students to graduate from Rains High School (the county's

only high school), she graduated third in her class. She was a member of the Beta Club (the honor society), the choir, treasurer of the senior class, Who's Who, and a UIL winner in shorthand during her senior year. Her favorite teacher, Mrs. Audie Shiflet, taught her shorthand. Mrs. Shiflet was very instrumental in causing her to pursue a career in teaching—majoring in business and teaching shorthand, just as Mrs. Shiflet had done.

From Rains High School, Gwendolyn attended and graduated from Henderson County Junior College (now Trinity Valley Community

College). After two years at Henderson County Junior College, she continued her education at East Texas State University (now Texas A & M Commerce) where she received a Bachelor's Degree in Business Education and a Master's Degree in Guidance.

Following in the footsteps of her father, Gwendolyn McMillan Lawe became a teacher in the Dallas Independent School District— teaching business subjects at Hillcrest High School. She later transferred to Thomas Jefferson High School, where she is today. As a business teacher at Thomas Jefferson High School, she has served as department chair, member of the Faculty Advisory Committee, Sponsor of the African American Culture Club, Student Council sponsor, Senior Class sponsor, served on the Ethnic Committee, and founded a mentor's program, which she received a grant from American Airlines. Because of rapid changes in technology, she now teaches computer classes (instead of shorthand, typing, etc.). She also teaches the computer segment of the Academy of Hospitality and Tourism at Thomas Jefferson High School.

Being a teacher is paramount in the writer's professional career; however, she co-founded and served as director of College Bound Tours. She conducted workshops and tours to Historically Black Colleges and Universities (HBCUs) for young people interested in attending college. She is also the co-founder of the A.C. McMillan Scholarship fund (in memory of her father), which gives scholarships annually to students at Rains High School.

Among her organizational affiliations include: member of Alpha Kappa Alpha Sorority, The Dallas Theater Center Guild, The African American Museum, New Hope Baptist Church, American Baptist Women, Classroom Teachers of Dallas/Texas State Teachers Association/National Education Association, Dallas Metroplex Council of Black College Alumni Associations, Texas Business

Teachers Association, Texas College Alumni Association, The NAACP (life member), South Dallas Business and Professional Women's Club, The Rains County Genealogical Society, Black Dallas Remembered, The East Texas Historical Association, and the National Trust for Historic Preservation. She also serves as the chairperson for the A.C. McMillan Scholarship Committee. Her volunteer work with these organizations and others is extensive.

Some of her awards and recognition include: winner of the NAACP Juanita Craft Award for Community Service, the Elks Award for Community Service, recognized as Outstanding Ex-Student/ Trinity Valley Community College (1992), and Community Service Award from the Dallas Metroplex Council of Black College Alumni Associations (1995). In 1999, Delta Sigma Theta Sorority honored her as "Teacher of the Year." In 2000, she was a winner of the "Women of Wonder," a national award given for community service by the Quaker Oats Company. She received a Visiting Professional Fellowship from the Smithsonian Institution and studied at the Smithsonian during the summer of 2003, in Washington, D.C. In 2004 and 2005, she was awarded a scholarship to attend the National Trust for Historic Preservation Annual Conference in Louisville, Kentucky, and Portland, Oregon, respectively. In 2007, she was recognized as a role model by Epsilon Sigma Chapter of Alpha Kappa Alpha, and in 2010 by the South Dallas Business and Professional Women's Club during Women's History.

Gwendolyn McMillan Lawe is married to Theodore M. Lawe, a Dallas entrepreneur and civic leader and the inspiration for her continuing the family history project. They live in Dallas, Texas ("on Wolfwood"). One daughter, Sylvia Gwen (Lawe) Williams and her husband Jerry and sons Preston and Blair live in Longview, Texas. Her mother, Modis McMillan, resides in Emory, Texas. She has three brothers, Alfred Clifton McMillan, Jewel Henry McMillan, and Harold Dale McMillan. Alfred resides in Emory; Jewel lives in Lake Jackson, Texas; and Harold and his son Hayes Michael live in Austin, Texas.